Co

A. G. STREET'S

Country Calendar

WITH AN INTRODUCTION BY
JOHN CHERRINGTON

ILLUSTRATED BY
LIONEL EDWARDS

Oxford New York
OXFORD UNIVERSITY PRESS
1986

Oxford University Press, Walton Street, Oxford OX2 6DP

Oxford New York Toronto
Delhi Bombay Calcutta Madras Karachi
Petaling Jaya Singapore Hong Kong Tokyo
Nairobi Dar es Salaam Cape Town
Melbourne Auckland

and associated companies in
Beirut Berlin Ibadan Nicosia

First published 1935 by Eyre & Spottiswoode Ltd
First issued as an Oxford University Press paperback with a new introduction 1986

British Library Cataloguing in Publication Data

Street, A. G.
[Country calendar]. A. G. Street's Country calendar.
1. Farm life—England—Wiltshire—History—20th century
2. Wiltshire—Social life and customs
I. [Country calendar] II. Title
942.3'1083'0924 S522.G7
ISBN 0-19-281930-5

Library of Congress Cataloging in Publication Data

Street, A. G. (Arthur George), 1892–1966.
A. G. Street's country calendar.
(Oxford paperbacks)
1. Street, A. G. (Arthur George), 1892–1966—Biography. 2. Authors, English—20th century—Biography. 3. Farmers—England—Wiltshire—Biography.
4. Farm life—England—Wiltshire. I. Title.
PR6037.T776Z463 1986 630'.92'4 [B] 86—5130
ISBN 0-19-281930-5 (pbk.)

Printed in Great Britain by
Richard Clay (The Chaucer Press) Ltd
Bungay, Suffolk

Contents

List of Illustrations

INTRODUCTION

by

JOHN CHERRINGTON

Arthur Street had more influence on my farming life than any other person. In early 1932 I was working on a large cattle estancia in Argentina when someone sent me *Farmer's Glory*. I was at the time debating whether to return to England or to go back to New Zealand, where I had lived four years before. At that time it was generally believed that English farming was finished, swamped by the production of the Dominions and the New World. In *Farmer's Glory* Street demonstrated in no uncertain way that it was possible to farm successfully in the southern England of the 1930s, provided one was prepared to work and disregard conventional practices.

This then was the first catalyst. The second was to turn my mind to Wiltshire. He convinced me that the chalk downs were crying out to be turned from arable to pasture grazed by dairy cows. My previous experience had been in Shropshire on traditionally good land, but where cattle had to be winter-housed. I had a job in Shropshire and the offer of a farm as well, but such was the attraction of the Wiltshire environment that he depicted that I bid farewell to Shropshire and in 1933 rented my first farm on the western edge of the chalk about ten miles from Arthur's own farm.

At that time I had never met him. He was famous and I was a very junior Wiltshireman, and in a couple of years I had to move to Hampshire. But there I continued with the same outdoor dairying which had saved him and supported me through those difficult pre-war years. Every week I read his column in *The*

Farmers Weekly. Very few writers can hold a farming readership, but he could express in terms that farmers could understand all the problems and prejudices that were, and still are, rife among us.

I seldom agreed with everything he said and, greatly daring, began putting pen to paper to contradict him and, in particular, commonly held assumptions of the farming establishment. Instead of squashing me as an impudent upstart or as a possible competitor, which is what I in my arrogance believed, he sought me out, became a friend and gave me good advice on how to deal with editors, radio producers and the like.

An editor, he told me once, is an idle fellow. Once he has a contributor who can fill his set column in the paper with moderately readable stuff, he puts it out of his mind and can turn to the next problem. So, said Arthur, demonstrate reliability and readability and you should get on. With Macdonald Hastings he edited *Country Fair* for a number of years and employed me to write a column. Neither of these were idle editors and they chased me relentlessly if I did not come up to their idea of scratch.

Where I was really far out of his class was in his descriptions of the Wiltshire scene. I don't know a single writer who could so accurately depict the Wiltshire dialect. I was farming in Wiltshire as *Country Calendar* was being written and the men I employed and the dealers and neighbours I met with all talked like it too. It was common to one and all and in time I came to imitate it to the extent of instructing my cowman to fetch 'thicce roan heifer from the big maid'. Today the dialect is almost gone but my old foreman, now retired, still uses it naturally, while the younger generation who have learnt to talk through the radio or television have sometimes difficulty in understanding him.

Street's farm-workers, gamekeepers, dealers, farmers and the landed classes are, it seems to me, drawn from life. Some of these were quite recognisable local characters, but painted with an over-kindly hand. I hardly know one character in his books whom one could dislike.

Even the village poacher-cum-poultry thief-cum-picker-up of unconsidered trifles can be looked on as an engaging rogue through Arthur's pen. But this is no more than his art. I was originally completely seduced by his characterisations into believing that the countryside was populated by the most kindly people, only too ready to give everyone a helping hand. There were, it is true, many such, but I soon found out that Wiltshire was just as much a jungle as any other society where the essential was to look after oneself.

But this was understandable. Street grew up at a time when British farming was being governed by the Cheap Food Policy which followed the repeal of the Corn Laws in the mid-nineteenth century. There were no barriers at all to the floods of imported food: wheat and barley from the New World; butter and lamb from New Zealand; beef from Argentina and so on. Whole areas of arable Britain were turned into deserts; thousands of farmers and their workers left the land.

Some farmers adapted and survived, but they had a struggle and were without mercy to their men or to their landlords, or to anyone else of whom they could take advantage. One well-known local farmer turned a dozen families off his thousand-acre farm, put up barbed wire fences and imported a Scottish shepherd with a dog to take their place.

It used to be the practice for farmers to supply their men with wheat or barley as part of their wages, and this they would take to the mill to be ground. Hearing that Scots farm-workers could exist on oatmeal porridge—a cheaper grain—some farmers supplied their Wiltshire labourers with the same, forgetting that porridge needs milk or cream or butter to make it a balanced human diet. Wages were abysmally low and the cottages for which they had to pay rent were no more than squalid rural slums. These conditions inevitably forced the more intelligent and independently minded of the countrymen to seek their fortunes elsewhere.

In many instances village life could be a tyranny, ruled by the squire, a large farmer or landlord. The countryman's life was much influenced by the parson, often an appendage of the big house. The village school was another pillar of the establishment. It was a well-ordered society for those who liked being ordered. The main catalyst of change was the nonconformist movement, but chapel folk were always spoken of contemptuously by the more orthodox.

Street grew up at a time when farming had adapted to the changing scene. It was not particularly profitable according to contemporary accounts, but much of Wiltshire had had the benefit of dairying, which did help farmers even before the First World War. He talks of the period as one of 'Glory', but I believe he was looking back through rose-coloured spectacles at a glory that never really was. In actual fact, the last period of real farm prosperity, when land prices reached their highest level, was in the 1860s before the floods of imported food arrived.

Although born on a farm he was not of traditional farming stock. His father was a grocer who took to farming, but he was a man of markedly independent views on politics and everything else. Arthur obviously inherited some of his father's independence and quite naturally cleared off to Canada as a young man as an alternative to fitting into the mould at home. This must have been an immense advantage to him as he developed an independence of mind and expression which might never have surfaced had he remained in England.

He took on the farm after his father died at the end of the

First World War. After the lift given to farming prosperity during the war the government of the day had promised legislation to guarantee the price of grain in the future—and promptly repudiated it. Street saw his investment of borrowed money lose steadily in value through the 1920s until, towards the end of that decade, he was practically insolvent.

Then two things happened. He took on the outdoor system of dairying, and he began to write. His dairy enterprise extended to retailing the milk in the local town, but it wasn't until his first book, *Farmer's Glory*, was published that he believed he was safe from bankruptcy. His farming friends of those days scoffed when he told them he was writing a book. No one they knew had ever got out of trouble by such simple means, but one of them told me he could always be relied upon to make a good speech.

This, I am sure, was the key to his success as a writer. His prose was as easy to read as his speeches were to listen to. When he writes he is addressing the reader as an audience of one. It is not a product of education; by his own account he made little mark at school and never laid claim to being any sort of intellectual.

His writing could be fairly divided between the narrative and the carefully constructed article for sale. *Farmer's Glory* succeeded because it was, in the main, a straightforward account of one man's struggle to survive. It was of course immensely enriched by his characterisation and illustration of his neighbours, but the real meat of it was there for those who knew the score and could understand and sympathise. One could say the same of *The Gentleman of the Party*, which was a story of the life and death of a Wiltshire farm worker written with great sympathy and much understanding.

His novels were always an entertaining read but never, in my view, reached the standard of the first two. But they were a reflection of the countryside and its goings on as he saw it. They are also worth reading as an account of the development of farming, in which he was involved until the end of his life. He was a practical farmer of average ability. Had he had the makings of a farming tycoon, as some men had even during the thirties, he would have been too busy to write; nor would he have had the financial pressure to make him do so.

In his introduction to *Country Calendar* he says that he is writing it to please himself. Well, this is true of any writer, even one desperate to earn the fees. But with his natural shrewdness he was able to turn out prose which might have pleased him, but which was angled to attract the reader as well. His pieces appealed both to the country dweller, still in those days mainly engaged in getting a living off the land, and to the townsman, perhaps of only one or two generations, who relished the nostalgia he provided.

Nowadays the world he described seems generations away. Few village dwellers have the least connection with farming, thanks to the contraction of the farm labour force over the last twenty or thirty years, which has been the direct result of the prosperity of farming. For farming *has* been prosperous, but as the basis of that prosperity entailed the high costs of mechanisation, land fertiliser and other inputs, so components that are not essential have had to be dispensed with. Since the Second World War between 3 and 5 per cent of the labour force has left the land annually.

They were not sacked for the most part, but they took jobs in towns, and communications being what they were then—scarce and expensive—they had to move nearer their work. The cottages, which in my young day used to be let for a few shillings a week, are now worth more than any farm-worker can afford to pay. Villagers these days are largely the retired, commuters and just a few farmers and workers, whose general outlook is completely alien to that of the majority.

In his later writing Street used to tell his farmer readers that they were the most unpopular people in Britain. Heavily subsidised, spoon-fed from the cradle to the grave. He died before the real attacks on modern farming got under way with their emphasis on the environment and the countryside, though like most farmers he did follow the latest developments as being essential for his farm's survival. His dairy herd was sold and he became a mechanised grain grower as it seemed the businesslike thing for him to do, though I don't remember him burning straw—probably because he was farming close to a straw-consuming area.

He could be very combative, both with the pen and with words, and it is a pity that *Country Calendar* contains so few examples of this. Perhaps as a good craftsman he was writing to capture a specific audience—the nostalgic successors of the real countrymen.

He had been a tenant farmer all his life, but he eventually bought a small farm on the outskirts of Salisbury. As he used to praise the landlord and tenant system in our arguments, I asked him what benefits and pleasure he stood to gain from this change of heart, since he still lived on his rented farm. 'Ah,' he said, 'the pleasure of finding you picking mushrooms in my field and telling you to get to hell out of it!' I can only say that landowners these days no longer shout at trespassers, whether they come from the local village or a town. Today's Englishman believes he owns the countryside and that farmers and the like are an anachronistic survival.

He had more influence on farmers and the general public than any writer of this present age. He was no agitator like Cobbett, nor faithful reporter like Arthur Young. There is no doubt that his greatest service to farming was that he did give the outside reader—and if one is not in it one is *very* outside—a fair picture of what farming at his time of writing was really like.

He never became a politician as far too many farmers do, but he was able to espouse a number of causes which he pursued with determination. At the same time as he was writing *Country Calendar* he was contributing a weekly column to *The Farmers Weekly*, and week after week he attacked the heavy four-bushel sack of wheat which farm labourers had to lift about. It weighed 2¼ cwt. and probably ruptured more men than anything else.

A whole industry supplying these sacks to farmers on a hire basis felt threatened, and counter-attacked as best they could. But he won in the end, and they exist no longer.

Then there were the horns on cattle, particularly Ayrshire cows. They injured the cowman, but far more frequently other cows in the herd. Now you hardly see a horned beast anywhere. Not long before he died he was fishing with me on the Test. I asked him how he would like to be remembered. 'As the man who got rid of the four-bushel sack and the horns off cattle,' he said.

Tangley Farm
December 1985

Author's Note

In common with the majority of farmers I allowed the unprecedented prosperity of those few years immediately following the Armistice of 1918 to go to my head, with disastrous results. A hefty bank balance and the prospect of a continuance of high prices for farm products made me forget the careful example and training of my parents to such an extent that I was no longer content to be just a tenant farmer, trying each year to put by a little for the inevitable rainy day. Like most of the younger generation, I knew a trick worth two of that. Rainy days were to be a thing of the past, and something between a wealthy country gentleman and a wealthy townsman seemed to be the ideal at which to aim.

But pride soon had a fall. By the end of 1922 I was well aware that the drop in price of all my produce meant that I was now living far beyond my income. Still, it seemed hardly worth while to alter my style of living because of one bad year. Things would be bound to take a turn for the better, and so, like a fool, I carried on as before. Besides, to cut down my personal expenditure to any appreciable extent would be merely advertising my hard-up condition to all my neighbours. When one's income increases how easy it is to adjust one's mode of life to match it! But when it decreases how difficult, well-nigh impossible, is the corresponding procedure!

Consequently, by 1927 my financial position was a desperate one, and I had visions of bankruptcy which were so clear and so recurrent that I could not sleep at nights. The thing that hurt most was that I was very conscious of how much better a start in life mine had been by comparison with my father's humble beginning, and that even with that great advantage here was I, at thirty-five, a failure. But was my present position too dire to alter? Was it possible for me to start again at thirty-five? Possible or not, I decided to have a shot at it.

The first thing to do was to try to cut my coat according to the cloth at my disposal in 1927, a very small amount; indeed, so small that a good many pleasant things had to be abandoned. Hunting, shooting, golf, holidays, and anything of like nature which cost money, all these had to be discarded in favour of hard work as a farmer. The immediate result of this pleased me greatly. Financially there is a world of difference between work and play. It works out something like a vote counting two on a division, for when you are at work, even though you may not be earning much money, you are spending none. So far, so good, I thought, and then I came up against another difficulty. While I found that I could substitute hard work on my farm for my one-time expensive daylight sports and pleasures, a costless and possibly profitable way of spending my evenings was not so easy to find. To go out anywhere would mean that I should spend money, and I had no money to spend. What could I do in the evenings?

Then came stroke of luck number one, in the extraordinary garb of a bout of influenza. I was recovering from this and had been downstairs for a couple of days, although I had not yet been allowed out, when one afternoon in November 1929 I chanced to read an article on farming's ills in the *Daily Mail*. This so annoyed me that I threw down the paper, saying aloud: "Why in the dickens doesn't somebody write the truth about farming?" My wife, who, I think, had had about enough of me lolling about the house all day, said: "Well, if you know so much about it, why don't you write one?" I took up this challenge—after all, even when a man is ill he should not let his wife bully him too severely—scribbled out just what I thought about the farming situation, and gave the result to her to read. Her criticism was as follows: "Of course, I don't know a lot about it, but if you were to take the bad language out of this it wouldn't be too bad." Just to show her, I took her advice and sent the finished product to Mr. P. W. D. Izzard of the *Daily Mail*, who, to my utter astonishment, not only printed it but paid me three guineas for it.

To a hard-up farmer this seemed too wonderful for words. Here was my evening occupation to perfection. Scribbling was interesting, it cost practically nothing, and it brought in cash. If in one hour I could earn three guineas, three hours each evening at the same rate of pay would soon put my little world straight again. But things did not work out quite in this fashion, although I went ahead with further writing right manfully. I bombarded Fleet Street with all sorts of things, and ninety-nine per cent. of my efforts were returned to me by the next post. Still, on looking up the figures I find that I earned eighteen pounds in 1930 and twenty-two pounds in 1931, not very rapid progress. But here was the great achievement—I had found a slightly profitable way of amusing myself during the evenings.

Then in the spring of 1931 came the second stroke of luck, this time in the guise of a good friend, Miss Edith Olivier. Having seen one of my efforts in the local paper, she called one day to suggest that I should write a book, bringing with her a copy of Mr. Adrian Bell's *Corduroy*.

"Read that," she said. "It is the story of a townsman turned farmer, and it's a fascinating book. You write one about farming from the inside, and you'll have an equally interesting one. I don't think that it has ever been done properly from the inside." And she left me that day with this parting advice: "Put it down just as it happened, and whatever you do, don't try to be clever."

When Miss Olivier had gone I thought over her suggestion.

By this time I had reached the age when one becomes aware that friendship is the most valuable thing in life, and her visit seemed to be an amazing illustration of this truth. Here was a friend who, very certainly, had nothing to gain by bothering with my amateur efforts at writing, taking the trouble to suggest a possible book, to lend me another as an example, to give me good advice, and to cheer me on to make the attempt. Here was the fine gold of friendship which must be accepted with sincere gratitude. The cuts in my personal expenditure and the corresponding increase in my farm work were already enabling me to scramble out of my financial hole, and the best way to repay my friend would be to make an honest attempt to act on her advice. And so I began to write my first book.

My household's attitude to this new occupation was, I suppose, natural enough under the circumstances, although it did not seem exactly helpful. When the day's farming was done, and I had retired into my den to scribble, I should imagine that their comments went something like this : " He's in there. He's quite safe. It pleases him, it keeps him out of mischief, it hurts nobody, and it costs nothing. When we think of what he might be doing we ought to be thankful for this new craze." They may, of course, have added : " Bless him ! " But it would be arrogant to say for certain that they did.

However, in spite of their general attitude of amused condescension to my new hobby, I persevered, and daily the book grew. Never before had I been so happy with a hobby. The whole business was fun, glorious fun, and, best of all, fun which cost nothing—blank paper, a stump of pencil, and the freedom to put down anything and everything which came into my mind. Of course, in spite of Miss Olivier's opinion, my scribblings would never be published, so I could write exactly as I liked. And then, miracle of miracles, my scribblings were published;

and now, some three years later, I find that my one-time hobby has become a serious business.

In many ways this is very pleasant, and I hope that I am sufficiently grateful to the Goddess of Luck, but, even so, when a hobby becomes one's work, part of the pleasure must disappear. For one thing I am naturally lazy, and I find that my writing must be done by myself. In farming, during any particularly busy time such as haymaking or harvest, one takes on extra men as required, but the scribbler must toil alone and unaided; and when he takes on this job in middle-age it comes hard. Gone is the amused tolerance of my household, and in its place is stern disapproval when I forsake my desk too frequently. In fact, to-day life is real and very earnest, or so I find it.

But the worst cross of all to bear is the ever-constant thought that now I cannot write exactly as I would like. How I wish that I could recapture the same carefree feeling which filled my mind during the writing of that first book. But to do so seems almost impossible. With the best goodwill in the world I cannot get out of my head the idea that, having written several books, I must now be careful when I set pencil to paper. I am well aware that this is a woefully mistaken attitude, but there it is —I am careful when I want to be carefree. So, for many months I have been thinking that when I have time I will write something to please myself, in order to try and recapture that glorious carefree state of mind once more.

" When I have time." That is a time which will never come, so I have decided to make time, and to begin this carefree writing this October. Somehow or other I will make time once a week at least to write something just to please myself in the hope that I may become as interested in doing it as I was in writing my first book.

COUNTRY CALENDAR

October

Somehow I think it fitting that these personal scribblings should begin in October, for, after all, I was a farmer long before I was a scribbler, and I still am a farmer, farming the farm on which I was born and bred—and the farmer's year begins in October. The townsman must obey the printed calendar; he may even pass laws affecting the setting of the mechanical clock, and so bamboozle himself daily; but the farmer must obey Nature's calendar, which she has printed and reprinted every year since Adam delved. The last edition of this is yet to come, and when it does come, of what use will be the townsman's calendar?

What a continuous round of planning for the future farming is! To-day, as I stood on the top of the down admiring the view of Wiltshire's spacious countryside, this thought came to me, for all round me was evidence of preparation for the future. Winter oats and barley were in and up, showing dark and light green patches on the far hillside. In one field I could see some men and horses busily wheat sowing, with some rooks in close attendance. In others ploughs were at work making lovely straight strips of chocolate over the landscape. Down the breeze came the stutter of a tractor, the "Whog awver, Vi'let," of a carter, and the rich hum of a threshing machine. The cows were still in green pastures; sheep bells tinkled in the distance; down in the water-meadows the drowner was busy preparing for some early Spring grass; in the buildings poultry and pigs were being fed and fattened; and in one place in the valley I could see the blue smoke of a hedger's fire ascending upwards to a clear blue sky. In that most wonderful setting, the English

In others, ploughs were at work.

countryside, the seemingly unhurried but continuous hustle of farming was going on according to ancient custom. Somehow or other it was a most satisfying picture.

* * * * * *

To-day I had occasion to drive to Bristol, or rather to drive through one of Nature's most glorious pictures, " Autumn in the West Country." The farmer's year may begin in the Fall when the ordinary year is dying, when Summer's glories have faded, when the fields are barren and shorn of their harvest, and when the leaves are beginning to fall ; but, even so, what a lovely land is the West of England at this season ! The trees were turning all colours—brown, dapple, cinnamon, russet, maroon, saffron, ruby, lemon, flame, khaki, steel-grey, and many other glorious shades, just like a catalogue of ladies' stockings. Refusing to think that soon all this beauty must patter to the ground with the coming of the frost, I drove along admiring the gorgeous colours of the trees as they showed serenely on a carpet of green, the green of our grass in the West. There is no green and no grass to come up to that in all the world. But I was forced to pay a compliment to Somerset this morning, for her grass is a wealthier green than ours in Wiltshire. I suppose the reason is that Somerset's subsoil is something different from my native chalk.

I drove home through the village of Priddy and came slowly down the Cheddar Gorge. How small those cliffs make one feel! I shall never forget my first sight of them some years ago when I drove some friends down between them late one summer night. There were four of us. We were all young, we had dined well, we were fit, irresponsible, and very merry. How we chattered and laughed and joked as we entered the Gorge!

About half-way down we stopped and got out of the car to smoke a cigarette. Soon the chattering and merriment ceased, for the majesty of those rugged crags showing clearly against the night sky overawed us all. Soon one of the party voiced the common thought: "Come on," he said, "let's get out of this. I want to go to a more kindly spot to restore my self-respect." The man who does not feel very humble occasionally before the face of Nature is past praying for.

* * * * * *

To-day brought its note of tragedy. A week or so ago twenty in-calf heifers arrived here from Ireland, and this morning I was compelled to shoot one of them to save her from further pain after a bad calving. Somehow, although I have been accustomed to shooting from boyhood, and look upon it as one of the natural amusements of country life, I hate doing this sort of thing. Consequently, when it has to be done I do it if I am available, for it is hardly fair to order a man to do something which one hates doing oneself. Rightly or wrongly, I can and do obtain pleasure from shooting all sorts of game birds and animals, but to shoot a sick animal is a very different proposition.

Always it looks at you so reproachfully and with such lack-lustre eyes as you glance down the barrels of your gun.

In this case it seemed that I was entirely responsible for the tragedy. What right have I, simply because I have the necessary money to invest in farming, to cause that heifer to leave her native country and experience a terrifying and uncomfortable journey by ship and train to my farm, only to die a few weeks later?

But it is all the luck of the game of life. Life is a gamble, and so is farming, and it is useless to be too sentimental over these happenings. Nature is often ruthless and cruel, and, farming being a natural thing, when you keep livestock, in the natural order of things you will occasionally have dead stock. Besides, the other heifers have been calving down satisfactorily, and I am sure, since I have not housed any cattle at night, that my losses from all causes have been considerably reduced. On the average in a herd of about a hundred milking cows I reckon to lose but two each year.

However, in order to get the taste of that business out of my mouth, I walked over to the water-meadows to commune with the drowner, a cheery soul. Many of the older farm labourers are, a thing which always makes me feel rather small whenever I come across an instance of it. These men have lived a hard life, in which there has been little or no ambition for material success, and in which there can have been very few luxuries or comforts. Yet who shall say that these men are failures? Rather would I point to them as being conspicuous successes, for they are happy men, and many others, although they may be possessed of both fame and fortune, are unhappy by comparison.

Anyway, Jim, my drowner, is a happy man, and a chat with him never fails to cheer me up. He is never bored, but always keenly interested, both in other folks' doings as well as his own.

World be badly off without a few of these old Stalwarts.

To-day he took me for a tour of the water-meadows, pointing out where he was making alterations and where he required planking for repairs.

" We've a got the meads well in 'and thease roun'," he remarked, " an' lookeezee, they be a tarble bit better than when I vust took 'em on. I 'low as I've a left me mark on 'em, as'll bide a year or two atter I be gone." Only a very small minority of mankind are able to say that in their old age, and to my mind it is a justifiable thing about which to boast. That was the old spirit behind farming in this country with both master and man, until forces outside their control set them off on the precarious path of trying to make money. Still, even to-day British farming would be badly off without a few of these old stalwarts who put the land on which they toil first and their own needs second.

Just before I left Jim this morning he switched on to an entirely different topic. In spite of the fact that, in his opinion, I spend far too much time at my desk and neglect my farming to some extent in consequence, he reads all my books and passes pungent criticism on every passage in them where, in his view, I have allowed my fancy to stray from the realms of possibility.

" I bought thic last book o' thine eesterday," he remarked firmly.

This was either a tribute to my powers as an author, or a subtle rebuke to my meanness in not presenting him with a copy, so I asked him what he thought of it.

" I bain't gwaine to buy no more o' thy books," he said gloomily.

" Why ? " I asked.

" Cause they do keep I up too late. I zit up wi' thic book till atter one las' night. Thic zart o' caper's no good to a 'ard-workin' man. Still, tain't a bad book, but you be a main bad speller. Leastways, you don't spell zame as I. Where's thee go to school?"

"In Wiltshire, Jim, same as you."

"H'm! Zo I thought. But I 'low tain't your fault. 'Tis they volk up in Lunnon wot cain't spell. They printers, an' sich like."

"But what's wrong, Jim?"

"There's a mistake in thic book. Lookeezee! 'Ow dost thee spell 'Drawings'? Thee's know, down in water-mead."

"DRAWINGS, Jim."

"An' zo do I, an' zo do iverybody wot 'ave bin to school proper. But in thic book 'tis spelled 'DROW.' You tell they printers an' yer publishers, too, that they've a let 'ee down. You wants to be more keerful wi' Lunnon volk. They cain't be trusted to do nothin' proper, cepts to vill their bellies wi' cheap vittles. Poorish tools they be. Thee tell 'em I zaid zo when you be up there next time. Now you'd best goo to yer work, an' lave I to clean out thease carriage. I've a wasted a main zight too much time wi' 'ee already 'smornin'."

It is useless to argue with a man like that, even if you do employ him, so I obeyed. But just wait, when I go up to town next week to lunch with "they poorish zart o' tools," namely my esteemed publishers, I shall "tell 'em proper."

* * * * * *

It is Michaelmas Day—or, rather, Old Michaelmas Day, October 11th, for New Michaelmas Day falls on September 29th. Thank goodness it is a gloriously fine day, for this day is the day on which all the farm labourers in this district who are changing jobs shift their goods and chattels from one cottage to another. A long journey through driving rain is bad for bedding and furniture, for quite a lot of this business is still done by the two-horse wagon, and the best of tarpaulins does not keep all the damp away.

Once again I have no changing on my farm. I have not hauled in the goods of a new man for some five years now, and we all seem so satisfied with each other that neither the men nor I bother about agreeing each Michaelmas for another year's work together. We seem to take it for granted that only death or some big upheaval in our lives which is beyond our control will terminate our relationship of master and man.

Which is all to the good, for what farming needs and what our countryside needs above all else is this sort of stability and continuity. When farms are repeatedly changing hands it is bad business for all concerned, landlords, farmers, labourers, and their wives and children. Countryfolk do not desire great wealth; rather they want stability and peace. They want to work and enjoy their work on the land which they know and love. It takes a lifetime to know a farm properly, and even when a man spends his whole life on one farm he is still learning in his last year.

To my mind, no matter what the reason, a farm sale is a depressing thing, and I rejoice that this year there have been fewer farm sales than for several years past. Even when the financial success of the quitting farmer is the cause—a very rare happening—his sale must mean a painful uprooting for a good many people. The incoming tenant will never engage all the old staff, and those whom he does not engage will have to seek new jobs, and, what is far worse, new homes. Besides, farmers and farm labourers are the trustees of that portion of the land of their own country which circumstances have placed in their care. It is bad business to change trustees of anything valuable too frequently.

That point about farm labourers being compelled to seek new homes when they quit their jobs is always a sore one, but the critics of the tied farm cottage should realise that it has some advantages to man as well as to master. For some years now the farm worker in regular employment has had a very cheap cottage at three shillings per week. I know this because my farm is short of cottages and some of my employees are compelled to rent a free cottage, nothing to do with the farm, at about eight shillings per week. Still, that all rural cottages are not tied to-day is undoubtedly an improvement on the old days when there were hardly any free cottages ; but under any system of farming, even under State farming, a certain proportion of cottages must go with the farm. The key men must live on top of their jobs, for farming never stops, day or night. For instance, you can't see in-calvers too often.

What a fitting word " Husbandry " is to describe farming ! The man who farms merely to rob the soil for his own material gain and who leaves his farm in a hopeless state of poverty and weeds does not know the meaning of the word. Neither is he playing his rightful part as a countryman in the nation's life. He is a traitor to his trust. A husband should love and care for his wife, and a farmer should do the same for his land. He should be in actual fact its husband, and practise good husbandry, leaving his land in better condition than he found it. That was the spirit behind farming in my boyhood. There should always be something more in farming than just making money, and I have a notion that the future will force the nation to recognise this eternal truth.

* * * * * *

The other day a friend gave me a copy of a book on farming which was written by a farmer, and published as far back as 1853. Its title is *Talpa, or the Chronicles of a Clay Farm*, and it contains the experiences of its author, Mr. Chandos Wren Hoskyns, while he was farming some of the stiff clay lands of Warwickshire. While all of its contents interested me greatly, I feel obliged to make a note here of one passage. In referring to the prevailing high price of wheat at the time, with its resultant bad farming, the author asks a brother farmer: "Will you pray that the inducement may continue of that style of farming? Of that style of competition? Of that style of rent raising, that ends in ruin to the beggared land, the ignorant landlord, the foolish tenant, and the defrauded labourer?" And when his neighbour asks how to stop the wheat-mining farmers, he answers: "By serving them as you do the Rats when you take the Ricks away! Starving 'em out! There's no *other* way! Their food—their only food is—ever has been—the *premium* price—the *disproportionate* value of the grain-crop. TAKE AWAY THAT BAUBLE!" The italics and capitals are the author's, not mine, although I say "Amen" to every one of them. To-day the position in the farming world is much the same. However, the Wheat Quota is here, for good or ill. Let us use it only in so far as wheat-growing works in with good farming. Let us grow wheat in its proper proportion, and refrain from over-cropping with this cereal simply because there seems to be some money for nothing attached to it. That must surely be the wish of everyone who has any real regard for the future of England's countryside.

Which reminds me that yesterday and to-day we put in seventeen acres of wheat on this farm. The weather was a trifle catchy with rain, but on the whole the seed went in well. "Barley in dust and wheat in mud" is an old saying which is still true in this district. It occurs to me that although I have been an all-grass farmer for several years, and although this method of farming has paid me and saved me, in the future I shall grow a little corn each year. One lives and learns, and in a very dry

season an all-grass farm in this chalk district grows too light a crop of hay. Each year to cash the fertility of one of my pastures which has been stored there by my livestock seems to me to be sound business. By so doing I shall obtain some straw for litter and thatch, and, as I intend to grass the field again with a temporary ley, I shall have a field of new seeds every year, and thus a good hay crop even in a drought. From 1929 to 1933 my farming was governed by " Permanent Pasture " ; in the future this will be altered to " Temporary Pasture," which will, I think, be a change for the better. Besides, this alteration will make my farming so much more interesting. Farming without a seed-time or a harvest is a dull, unromantic business, even though it may be a profitable one.

*   *   *   *   *   *

Recently we have had quite a lot of rain, for which many thanks. The countryside needed it, and, for once, the desires of both town and country were agreed. This morning, in a steady drizzle, I went to the local Ploughing Match. During the past ten years much of this district has gone down to grass, but we have still quite a lot of arable. In a large field of wheat-stubble near Salisbury ploughs of all kinds were busily at work—single-furrow ploughs drawn by two horses, double-furrow ploughs drawn by three horses abreast, and tractor-ploughs, some of them up to four furrows. The first type, the single-furrow, is the least economical, but no one will dispute when I say it is the most beautiful. The three-horse team looks unwieldy by comparison, and the tractor is only a mechanical noise—it possesses little beauty or romance. However, the ingenuity of man has contrived efficient tractors and efficient ploughs for them to haul, and the work done by the tractor ploughs to-day compared very favourably with the single-plough work in quality, while in quantity the tractors won in a canter, or rather in a buzz.

There is more beauty in the plough than in any other farm implement, and, even in these days when British farmers have wisely reduced their ploughing land in the face of the increasing competition in grain-growing from overseas, the sight of a ploughing match must give the most hardened grass farmer a thrill. All those teams of good horses, groomed to a fine gloss, working in their best harness, and decked with bells and brasses, toiling steadily and straightly over one of the mellowed fields of England—is there any sight to beat it? Even the tractors, ugly and noisy though they be, seem less ugly and less noisy in such a spacious setting. Landlords, farmers, and labourers, walking up and down the ridges, watching and criticising the work; Salisbury spire tapering in a grey sky on one side of the scene, and the Wiltshire downs showing solid and stable through the misty rain on the other; the whole thing was a bit of the real England, the England I love best.

Naturally I was chaffed by my neighbours for my appearance at a ploughing match. They welcomed me as a long-lost sheep returning to the fold. Somehow or other many of them have got it into their heads that I want to see an all-grass England. I do not, and so I told them. I want to see a prosperous countryside in this country, and in these days that must mean, as it has meant for many years, a large proportion of grass land, as only in livestock farming can we hope to compete with the overseas farmer and keep our land in good heart. I do not want to see more acres of wheat grown here; I want to see heavier crops on the existing acreage.

Besides, who are they to be surprised at my going to a ploughing match? I have been a ploughman, both in this country and Canada. If I am not mistaken, I have ploughed more acres myself than most of my neighbours, and, even if it sounds like blowing my own trumpet, I was, and could be to-day if occasion arose, a good ploughman, both with horses and tractor. Sometimes I think that the happiest days of my life were those long, lonely days over twenty years ago when I followed a breaking-plough in North-west Manitoba.

But now I am too old—or, rather, too lazy—to "hold plough," either for toil or pleasure, and scribble for the former and play games in pursuit of the latter. After lunch to-day I played golf, and it rained pouring throughout the round, thank goodness! I say that because I am not a good golfer; I cannot stop a ball on a hard green. This afternoon the approach shots stopped where they fell, and I won my match together with its heavy monetary stake—the value of one glass of beer. Is there any drink which comes up to that hard-won glass at the end of eighteen holes, or any hot bath so pleasant as that which follows getting wet through during some country pastime? I do not think so. The one is pure nectar, and the other is pure bliss.

No matter what may be said against golf and those who play this game, I, for one, derive great good as well as great pleasure from it. For a fairly busy man of middle-age it seems to fill the bill most excellently. Its greatest advantages are that to play it satisfactorily does not necessitate a crowd, and that while one is engaged in a round one is safe. I do not mean merely safe from the calls of one's business or domestic cares, but also safe from the nagging of one's own thoughts. Often some of my writing work comes hard ; after all, I am only a glorified amateur, and sometimes an article which has to be in the night post simply won't get itself written satisfactorily. A year or two ago I used to sweat blood when this happened, but now I do not worry, for golf has found the way out. After a morning of hard work and gloom with only a few hundred words of poor stuff to show for it, I slip away to the golf course. There, in the interest of trying to make my friend and opponent pay for my drink, I forget all my cares. I forget that I have to write an article before eight o'clock, I forget that I have a farm or a typewriter, and, if truth be told, I forget sometimes that I have a wife and child. All my energies, both physical and mental, are concentrated on this confounded game of golf which looks so easy but which I find so difficult. For two glorious hours everything else in the world does not matter a hoot. Then, in the evening, I find that the article just writes itself, and the beneficial effect of those two hours of mental fallow is shown in the ensuing crop.

* * * * * *

I have just returned from a week-end in Norfolk. For several months some of my farming friends in the north-west of that county had been daring me to pay them a visit, and my Wiltshire farming friends had been saying that if I took the dare I should be lucky if I returned home with a whole skin. On both counts, therefore, a visit to Norfolk had to be paid—one can ignore the sneers of enemies quite cheerfully, but the chaff of friends is a more serious matter.

From the conversation at the dinner-table on the first evening I gathered that my great crime against Norfolk is that I, a mere Southerner, have dared to criticise this county in any way whatsoever. Apparently Norfolk is beyond criticism, and my hosts did their best during my stay to show me the error of my ways. They did more—they invited their many friends to lunch and dinner and tea in order that they might help in the good work, and they took me by car and on foot over acres and acres of Norfolk's farming.

In one thing they failed to change my views about Norfolk, and that is concerning its comparative isolation from the traffic of the nation. Undoubtedly Norfolk is what we in Wiltshire call " side-off," for the main route from North to South, either by road or rail, misses it completely, and, apart from the sugar-beet industry, factories are few and far between. Norfolk is a farming county. There one talks farming, thinks farming, dreams farming, and lives farming almost to the exclusion of all else; but the only farming which is considered worthy of notice is the type of farming which has been carried on in Norfolk from time immemorial. Change—any change—even a change for the better—is regretted. Even where a change in farming methods has proved profitable, the farmer concerned does not love it. " Fancy me, a Norfolk farmer, having anything to do with things like Asparagus and Brussels Sprouts ! " is the prevailing attitude.

It is easy to see why this part of England has been able, most unfairly in my opinion, to decide the agricultural policy of Great Britain. Nowhere have the large landlords shouldered the burden of the post-War agricultural depression to such an extent as in Norfolk. Farms, good farms, have been greatly and repeatedly reduced in rental, and in numerous cases have been let rent free. Here the relationship between landlord and tenant is the most intimate I have ever come across, both parties knowing the smallest details of each other's difficulties. It seemed to me that, in a vain attempt to preserve the rural and almost feudal life of Norfolk unchanged, the Norfolk landlords have sacrificed themselves in order almost to spoon-feed and nurse their tenants. While to my mind this was mistaken kindness in many cases, one must give honour where honour is undoubtedly due. Still, my visit confirmed one thing beyond all question; the collapse of meat prices had a great deal more to do with Norfolk's farming troubles than the fall in grain prices.

Another impression I gathered during my stay was that Norfolk's farming community—which, by the way, comprises everybody—does not approve of interlopers from other parts of Great Britain, and especially when these aliens make a success of their farming. One has to be born and bred in Norfolk to fit in properly, and I should imagine that it would take at least three generations before one really belonged. Norfolk wants a condition of things in which shooting and hunting *ad lib.* will work in with profitable farming, and that day, alas! seems to have gone for ever. That is why the hard-bitten interloping farmer, who cares for none of these things, but only for the profit and loss account of his farming, does not fit very happily. All crimes, troubles, and sins, both of omission and commission, are traced to the successful alien farmer, and I hope, for his sake, that no one will perpetrate a trunk murder in Norfolk. If this should occur, everybody in the district would point to the nearest interloper as the culprit, and a Norfolk jury would hang him out of hand. Still, these newcomers will increase in numbers in the near future most probably, because in Norfolk there is a considerable acreage of good level land, which, from what I could gather, can be rented very reasonably, the only drawback being that it must be farmed in accordance with the Norfolk tradition. But somehow I don't think that I shall ever attempt to do this, for barbed-wire fences and water-troughs—conspicuous by their absence on the farms I walked over—would be sure to bring black looks from all sides, and I have reached the age when I want to live amicably with my neighbours.

But what a lovely unspoilt land Norfolk is! Modern civilisation, with its hustle and bustle and noise, seems to have passed it by. Buses are comparatively few and far between; cars seem to recognise that other people, even people walking with three or four puppies, have a right to the road; a serene peace seems to brood over the countryside; farming comes first, last, and all the time; and everybody, from the Squire downwards, has a genuine love for the land. It was this last which my hosts and I had in common, and it was this, I fancy, which enabled us to argue fiercely about farming policy during every waking moment of my stay, and still to remain good friends. To travel is to learn, willy-nilly, and one result of my visit is that now I have a better knowledge of Norfolk's difficulties and a much higher opinion of Norfolk's countryside and its dwellers. Also I am daring to hope that some of them may say that the interloper for one most enjoyable and friendly week-end was not so bad as he had been painted.

* * * * * *

Home again. The cobbler says that there is nothing like leather, and every countryman says the same about the district in which he was born and bred. To-day I have been farming—hard. Every man can be done without, a fact which death proves to someone or other at every hour, but while we live we hate to think this about ourselves. At any rate, I hate to do so. My men are capable and conscientious, but I had been away for five whole days, and, no matter how efficacious animal or artificial manure may be, I still hold that " the master's foot is the best dung." Consequently, to-day the master's foot travelled over almost every field on this farm.

Every man has his secret desire, I suppose, and mine is some day to own a farm. My walking to-day was very pleasant indeed, but how much more so would it have been if every time I put my foot down I could have said " Mine ! " I know that such thoughts are foolish. I know—and even if I did not know my friends tell me so in no uncertain voice—that I am probably much better off as a tenant of this farm than I should be as its owner, or the owner of any other farm in this district, but still I hanker to plod along over the fields saying : " Mine, mine, mine." This is not a popular thing to admit, but there it is. In common with most men I yield to the natural lust to own absolute dominion over some of the mellowed fields of England. My wife implores me not to think of doing anything so fat-headed as to buy a farm. " Now that at long last we are feeling almost financially secure for the first time since we married," she says, " why spoil it ? Why put our heads into another financial noose ? " My best friend says the same thing in more forcible language. " You bide put, an' don't be a b—— fool," is his way of putting it. He goes even further. He says : " And mind, I won't let you be one if you want to. If you won't listen to reason, I'll come and knock some sense into your thick head."

Of course, I know that both my wife and he are quite right : I know that I should be a fool to buy a farm as long as I can bide put ; but I know also that some day I shall try to commit this foolishness, even though I am certain that I shall regret doing it. Man is rarely a logical animal at the best of times, and this business does not admit of logic, anyway. I don't want good advice : I want to own some land. And some day I have a notion that I shall own some, although the how and the why and the when and the where are beyond my ken.

But to get back to my farming. All was well. Not even the most disgruntled farmer could have found to the contrary. The cows were milking well, the winter wheat was well up in drill, there was still a plenteous supply of grass keep, and the farming year seemed to be away to a good start. Visiting other districts is interesting and very enjoyable, but home is home. I know this district like the palm of my hand. Every tree, every bush, every fold in the landscape, every bend in the river Wylye, and every curve of the downs hold memories of joy and sorrow, of defeat and success. My Norfolk friends will be saying the same about their home land. No matter where you go in this green island, either to farm in or to look at the countryside takes some beating.

November

Willy-nilly the job of writing about farming has devolved upon me, so in order to extend my knowledge I accepted an invitation from a friend to visit Scotland, and for two days I have been driving steadily northwards. Driving alone like this, one obtains a much better impression of the size of our farming industry, for one passes through so much more countryside than town. In fact, the towns seem to be just incidental dots of something different. It is true that a red straggle of ribbon-building is creeping out from them along the main roads, but when once this has been left behind, it is farming, farming, farming, all the way on either side of the road.

Berkshire and a little of Oxfordshire seemed to be very like my native county of Wilts, but then came the grass and hunting country of Northants and Leicestershire ; and as I journeyed northwards, so did the corn land diminish and grass and stock farming increase, while the corn ricks got smaller and smaller. The wetter the climate, the smaller the corn rick and the better the thatching. In one farmyard in Yorkshire I saw a bunch of ricks which had not one straw out of place. They were perfectly round and perfectly thatched, and looked almost like the toy ricks of a child's farmyard. What a pity it is that such craftsmanship is dying out, simply and solely because, generally speaking, it does not pay ! Still, when one does come across it, one can rejoice that here is one farmer who is able to take a pride in his farming even at the expense of his pocket.

But all the countryside I passed through was lovely until I crossed the Yorkshire boundary into Durham, where man's industries had smudged the green landscape horribly. It was a relief to get through Newcastle and find unspoilt countryside once again, for Northumberland, a county of sheep, is a very lovely land indeed. Next came Berwick-on-Tweed, and then I was in Scotland for the first time in my life. From there to Edinburgh the plough was much more in evidence, and the land rightly deserved its use—good gutty land, well farmed, with livestock and potatoes battling for pride of place.

This evening my host informed me that my stay in Scotland was to be a busman's holiday, and that we were to go farming all day and every day, and talk about farming every evening. Still, he did ask me whether I had brought my golf clubs, so evidently there is to be a little relaxation fitted in sometimes. Methodical dogs, these Scots. He put before me a definite programme for the coming week. To-morrow we are to visit a large dairy farm, next day a sheep farm, next a potato farm, and so on. Golf is to be worked into this journeying at intervals, and discussion of farming politics as they affect Scotland is to garnish the whole procedure. If I am not careful I shall return to Wiltshire in a kilt. Motoring makes me very sleepy, and as it is now midnight and I have to keep pace with these hardy Scots during a long day to-morrow, bed is indicated.

* * * * * *

This week in Scotland has been a crowded week of most interesting things. Farms of all kinds have I visited, for my host has torn up all the South of Scotland on my behalf. Somehow, up here farming seems to be a more honourable occupation than it is in England, for it is not looked upon as the one industry in which the fool of the family can make a success. Doctors, barristers, scientists, and other professional men have taken to farming in considerable numbers. I don't mean that they have retired from their professions to play at farming in their old age, but that they have abandoned their professions in youthful middle-age to take up farming.

And, by gum! they do farm. I do not know whether the difference in climate, the difference in nationality, or something else is responsible for their energy, but I must confess that the Scottish farmer and farm labourer work harder than their South of England counterparts. I admire and respect them for this, but I prefer to farm in the lazier district, for with the Scottish farming community it is a case of "force put" being "no choice." If they did not work harder than we do in the South they would never get a living.

On one farm I walked miles and miles in the driving rain over country that did not look worth a damn for any purpose. This was on the Lammermuirs, where by dint of toil and struggle through several generations a family of farmers had literally torn a good farm out of barren moorland. The farm consisted of several thousand acres, still chiefly moorland, but from the top of the hills one could see nearly a thousand acres of good grass and arable around the farmhouse and buildings, land which had at one time been in the same useless state as the bulk of the farm. When it no longer paid to effect this transformation the farmer's efforts ceased, and in one place a stone wall jutting out from the cultivated part into barren country showed the stopping place. Working for the state or for the community is all very well but it is difficult to improve land with only an idealistic motive. Individualism is supposed to be dying a natural death in these days, but for many years yet the driving force in farming will be the hope of reward that sweetens labour.

But Scottish farming was not all toil and sweat, I discovered. One day my host drove me southwards to the Cheviot Hills. At Jedburgh we left the main road and drove for about eight miles through a narrow valley. Along its middle babbled a burn,

a Britain of towns and factories seemed far away

which was bordered on either side by narrow green pastures—such bright green pastures! On the hillsides the green merged into the brown of bracken, and above this the brown faded to white, for the tops of the Cheviots were capped with snow. Sheep were dotted about everywhere, but for several miles we saw no human habitation, and only one human being, a lone shepherd standing by the burn watching our car in curious wonderment. Then suddenly, round a bend the road ended, and there were a clump of trees, a large farmhouse, two cottages, and a farm-steading, with the Cheviots frowning down on them from all sides.

Where the road ends—that in itself points out that passers-by are non-existent. This little cluster of buildings, set in a bright green pocket and surrounded by snow-capped hills, was the veritable back of beyond. And there in this oasis of green peace we spent the night and next day, our host being a sheep farmer. But this is hardly telling the truth about him or even doing him justice, for in reality he merited the title of " sheep baron ";

and in essentials he differed but little from his forebears who raided south into Northumberland when stock was scarce at home and a favourable opportunity for this pastime presented itself.

Here, as I say, the forceful bustle of Scottish farming was conspicuous by its absence, and here it was more than sufficient bliss just to enjoy the peace and beauty of one's surroundings. The Britain of towns and cars and factories and crowds seemed to be very far away, and neither I nor my companions seemed to miss it. We talked farming and sheep and hunting, and we revelled in the glorious privacy. Here the farmer is supreme overlord of his extensive domain, and the trespasser and the tourist bother him but little. But again I came up against that fact which so many townsfolk seem to ignore, that farming requires capital, for our host told me that he had over forty thousand pounds invested in his farming. Most folk who possess half that sum would not choose to live as he does on that Border farm, but rarely have I envied a man so wholeheartedly. There seemed to be something almost biblical in his life. Was it Abraham who had cattle on a thousand hills many years ago? Well, this man had Cheviot sheep on every hill in his sight. I imagine that at shearing time, lambing time, and during bad weather his leisurely existence is changed out of all recognition, but as I saw it during November it was good enough for me. Never have I enjoyed a short visit so much, never have I received such a kindly welcome, and never have I regretted saying good-bye to anybody or any place more than I did to my Cheviot host and hostess and their lovely Border homestead.

* * * * * *

Home again safe and sound, being able to say quite truthfully that my old car had carried me well during my Scottish holiday. Next morning when I looked out of the bathroom window I saw two sheep in the cowyard. As I don't keep any sheep this was evidence that the master's eye was needed. What in the world were two sheep doing in my yard? Seeing the dairyman in the lane I shouted to him, and he came along under the window. He told me that the two sheep—both shearling rams by the way—had wandered down the road a week ago, and that he had turned them into the yard.

"Have you told the police?" I asked, thinking that this would have been forgotten in my absence.

Apparently he had done so, but the police had not yet discovered the owner, so I made a note to ring up the Police Station when I got downstairs. But before I could do this I was scolded by my wife, who informed me in acid tones that anyone within half a mile would know I was back because of my bellowing. This shouting habit of mine is a sore point between us, but I cannot break myself of it. All farmers shout, and, when this proves unavailing, they bellow. There is some excuse for this because most of their conversation with their men has to be carried on against the noise of machinery, animals, or wind; and more often than not a good shout will save both time and walking. Besides, although farming may seem to be a leisurely business to many folk, in its actual operations there is no time to argue. For instance, if I saw a boy taking off a horse's bridle while the animal was hitched into a cart or wagon, I should bellow at him to stop; for, by the time I had walked across near enough to talk quietly to him, the horse would be galloping down the road, endangering other people and my property.

Still, I think that a lot of the misunderstanding and animosity between townsfolk and farmers—for there is animosity—is due to our habit of shouting. In ignorance that they are doing any damage, some townsfolk walk across a field or some town children swing on a wire fence, and then, as sure as fate, from about four hundred yards' range a raucous rural voice bellows at them to desist. No one likes being shouted at, and the result is that the shoutees return to town vowing vengeance which they effect by buying imported foodstuffs. Maybe this is an over-drawn picture, but I am certain that most farmers shout, and that being shouted at raises most people's worst passions.

But to return to my two visitors. In due course I rang up the police, who told me that they could not find anyone in the district who had lost two rams. I waited another week, and tried them again with the same result.

"Look here," I said, "how long am I supposed to keep the blame things? They're an infernal nuisance."

They said that they did not know, and when I threatened to turn the rams out into the road, they told me I should be prosecuted for permitting my animals to stray on the public highway.

"But they aren't my animals," I protested. "You jolly well buck up and find their owner."

It is rather curious, but although the police emulated the politicians and explored every avenue, they could not find an owner for my visitors, and a week or two later they told me that I could sell them. Accordingly, I sold them to a dealer friend, who picked them up in a motor-lorry one afternoon, and I imagined that in the course of forty-eight hours my waifs and strays would be very tough mutton. But not a bit of it, for next day my friend rang up to say that he had lost them. His conversation over the telephone is always a joy to listen to, and here it is.

"That you, Arthur?"

"Yes, Tom."

"You know they two sheep wot I picked up yesterday. Wall, I've a lost they. They be travellers, they be. The lorry come 'ome late an' we turned 'em into a paddock, an' next mornin' they jist werden there."

"But they can't have gone far, Tom," I chuckled. "Haven't you heard trace of them?"

"Naw! They be jist vanished. I 'low they be tourin' the South. I've a rung up everybody, an' I've a drove round lookin' fer 'em, but 'tis no go. One veller claimed five bob cause 'ee said as 'ow they'd eat his sprouts, but 'ee couldn' produce the culprits, zo I telled him, 'No sheep, no pay.' It don't look as though I be gwaine to make much out o' they, do it? You know, I doan' reckon they be sheep at all. I 'low 'tis a couple o' 'ikers wot 'ave mislaid thur shorts. Anyhow, when I do ketch 'em they wunt want neether shorts neet shirt. Dall it, I wish I 'adn' paid 'ee fur 'em, but you do allus do I. I say, do 'ee want a bunch o' good springers cheap?"

I think this "doing" business is carried out on a fifty-fifty basis between us, for I bought his heifers by telephone, and a day or two later he rang me up to say that he had found the hikers, and that they would not stray any more. Whether both he and I will be hanged for sheep-stealing in the near future as a result of this bit of business I do not know; but anyway I shall not enter the return from my only sheep-farming this year in my farm accounts. Any profit from those sheep must surely come under the heading of fortuitous receipts.

* * * * * *

It is curious how being pitied annoys one. During the Spring and Summer my town friends envy me my rural existence, but the other day while I was in London I found that they pitied me for being compelled to live in the country during the Winter. A dull, drizzly cold day seemed to give point to their arguments, and apparently all townsfolk hate the month of November. To them the other Winter months have certain virtues. October is often as genial as September; December brings Christmas, a time of joy and good cheer in any country and in any weather; January marks the New Year, a time of hope in spite of first instalments of Income Tax; February always grants a day or two of Spring; and March, in spite of its cold bluster, brings the daffodil and many other signs that Winter is over. But November has no redeeming feature. The days are short and dark, the weather is usually bad, and few townsfolk can find a good word to say for it.

Well, to the townsman November in the country may mean just mud and rain and clouds, but, even so, neither I nor anyone who lives and works in the country needs their pity. We know the countryside and the weather in all their varying moods, and know also that even the dark days of November have their charms. Not the least of these is the fact that the town visitor, the hiker, the caravanner, the picnicker, the trespasser, and all other intruders and disturbers of the rural scene have departed to their winter quarters. Road traffic is down by more than half, and the discordant notes of the gramophone, the wireless set, the motor-bike, and the motor-horn are no longer heard from the downs to the river from daylight until after dark. Instead, the countryside is peopled only by those who belong to it, and in consequence a natural pleasing quiet reigns over it once more.

In common with, I think, most of my neighbours, I revel in this state of things. Once again we have the countryside all to ourselves. No matter what the weather, we can work or play undisturbed, and that is why we enjoy and appreciate the privacy which November brings. The days may be short and dark, there may be rainy days, misty days, and windy days, but

peopled by only those who belong to it.

we know that November also brings us its quota—a fashionable word just now—of pleasant sunny days. November sunshine may not be so bright as that of June, but the air is clearer now. The rains have washed the blue haze from it, and the sky is a limpid, lucid blue. On a fine November day it seems as though the winds and rains which have preceded it have washed and purified both earth and air of all their summer humours, and cleansed them from all taint of mankind and his inventions.

Amidst all this peace and privacy farming makes haste slowly according to ancient custom. Land is ploughed, seed is sown, livestock are tended, and numerous other preparations are made for the future. No matter what the weather, the business of the countryside never stops, and in this month those engaged in it manage to enjoy some good sport. Shooting and hunting are now at their best, and for those who cannot afford the pheasant or the fox, there are the rabbit, the rat, and the wily wood-pigeon. The man who hacks home through the clean evening mist after a good day's hunting, the man who plods back over sodden ground laden with the spoil of a day's ferreting, and the man who waits for pigeons in the gathering dusk, none of these will grouse at dark November.

Neither will the majority of countryfolk, and the reason is twofold. Firstly, because they know that November is a time of purification, and that its winds and rains and fogs help to make possible the beauty of Spring and the bounty of Summer; and secondly, because either at work or at play they appreciate the rural privacy which dark November brings. And here one countryman reaches for his pouch.

*　*　*　*　*　*

I came across a rather unusual aspect of the dairying side of farming to-day. At ten-thirty this morning, as I was driving through a nearby village, I noticed two motor-cars bedecked with white ribbon buzzing about very busily. Chancing to meet a friend, I asked him whether the morning was the usual time for weddings in his village. "No," he said, "we generally do that sort of thing in the afternoon, but in this case 'tis a small-holder getting spliced, and he has to get that little job over in time to milk his cows at half-past two."

As I drove on my way all sorts of things came into my mind in connection with this explanation. When one thinks of a herd of cows ambling slowly along a lane, with one or two stopping every now and again to have a bite of grass from the bank, dairying seems to be a very leisurely business; but apparently it will not allow its servants much free time, not even to get married. That bottle of milk which appears so regularly on one's doorstep every morning does not arrive there without a deal of work and striving on the part of a good many people.

But surely, I thought, a man should be able to get a clear day off for such an important occasion as his marriage, even if he is a dairyman? Then the real reason for this hurried wedding came to me, the key being that the bridegroom was a small-holder. An employee would get the day off, most likely a clear week at his employer's expense, but a small-holder is a master man. He can take only the holidays which he can afford, and when he takes one he must pay somebody else to milk his cows. Still, they are *his* cows—that is, or should be, sufficient consolation—and I think it is that feeling of pride in ownership and being able to call no man his master which compensates the average small-holder for having to work so much harder and for so many more hours per week than the average farm labourer; for the difference in their weekly income is a very small one save in exceptional cases.

* * * * * *

In season and out I have been preaching that even a highly industrialised nation such as ours needs a prosperous rural countryside and community to form the necessary stable background to town life, and the other day I came across something which showed that one townsman at any rate valued country life as much for its unchanging stability as for anything else. I was having tea in a Gloucestershire farmhouse. The house and farm had been in my host's family for generations. They had never owned the place, but had farmed it as tenant farmers for so long that they almost looked upon it as their own. One of my host's brothers had left home many years before to earn his living as a townsman, but my hostess told me that when he came for a holiday to the old home he treated it just as though he were still a boy.

" Only this summer," she said, " he came through from the kitchen to the dining-room one afternoon and said to me: 'Mary, there's no string in the left-hand drawer of the kitchen dresser. Why? The string's always been kept there.' I tell you, Mr. Street, I suffer hardly from my husband's brothers."

Of course I sympathised with the lady sincerely and honestly, but all the time I could not help thinking that the incident illustrated the real value of rural life, a thing which can best be described in one word—permanence. Town is one buzz of movement and change, but the countryside stays put, or rather used to stay put. This man had spent his life in a large city ever since he had left his rural home in boyhood; he was a father, and a grandfather; he had achieved considerable business success, in doing which he had become a townsman to all external appearances; but still he looked upon that old farmhouse and its surroundings as the one really permanent thing in his life. Consequently, he felt aggrieved when this had let him down even in so small a matter as a change in the hiding-place of that useful article, a piece of string. It was the first sign of a crack in the stable background of his life.

I was telling this to a very modern town friend to-day, saying that people could bear the hustle and bustle of town life only while they knew that the stable peaceful background of rural life existed at their back doors, and that most of them did not wish our countryside to change much, if at all. " Rubbish! " he said. " You're becoming hopelessly old-fashioned and out of date. In a few years we shall need neither villages, farmhouses, nor string. We shall all live in large buildings of communal flats, which will be fitted with every known contrivance for our comfort and pleasure."

" When that happens, my bonny boy," I replied, " we shall be, in truth, a nation of flats."

* * * * * *

I have long felt that many of our national troubles are due to the fact that our administrators and their advisers live their lives too far away from the people to whom their decisions mean so much. In consequence, that blessed word " rationalisation " bears great responsibility. It is so easy to prove things, on paper; so easy to find a solution to any equation, on paper; but in actual practice one comes up against numerous factors which do not appear on paper, squared, or plain, or printed. For instance, one might be able to prove on paper quite clearly that it would be better for the boot trade, say, if ten per cent. of its factories were closed down. But what of the people who were employed in those closed factories? You cannot close down their lives and the lives of their families.

Recently there has been a proposal mooted in the Wiltshire County Council that the village of Martin, which is just over the county border in Hampshire, should be taken into Wiltshire. It lies in a small acute corner of Hampshire which juts into Wilts, and presumably the idea is to straighten the boundary between the two counties in order to make for more easy administration. At any rate so it would appear on paper—or, rather, on the map. Another reason for the Wiltshire authorities coveting this village is perhaps because it is the Winterbourne Bishop in W. H. Hudson's great book *A Shepherd's Life*; and yet another may be the desire to increase the size of Wiltshire merely out of pride. Anyway, one would imagine that few people would find much cause to object to the proposed change, for whether in Wilts or Hants, Martin will surely be able to carry on in much the same fashion as before, even though a change on paper has taken place!

Why then is there such strong opposition from Martin's inhabitants to this proposal? Simply because Hampshire is in the Southern Region while Wiltshire is in the Mid-Western Region under the Milk Marketing Board, which decrees that milk produced in Hampshire shall be worth at least one penny per gallon more than milk produced in Wiltshire. Consequently, to take Martin into Wilts will mean considerable money loss per annum to all the farmers in the parish. As one of my friends puts it: "What looks all right to a lot o' blamed officials in an office, means fifty bob a year less from every cow in Martin parish. And I 'low there's nigh on a couple of hundred cows there."

If one carries that a bit farther it is easy to see that one result of another scheme which looks admirable on paper is that farms in Hampshire are now worth more money, either to buy or to rent, while farms in Wiltshire must be worth less by a corresponding amount. Any attempt to stabilise our dairying industry on a profitable basis has my wholehearted sympathy, but I doubt whether the authors of the Milk Marketing Scheme realised what a great effect its working would have on land values throughout the country. The trouble is that in the majority of cases the incomes of all those connected with the administrative side of society are unaffected by the rules and regulations they bring into being. Take those county officials who want to put Martin into Wilts. With Martin in either county their incomes will remain the same, but to a farmer in Martin parish who is milking sixty cows this proposed alteration on the map will mean a deduction of one hundred and fifty pounds per annum from his takings.

This seems a gloomy entry to wind up November, which this year has been the reverse of gloomy with regard to weather. Besides, as yet, Martin is still in Hants, and I know that there are quite a few hard-bitten folk on the County Council who will put up a good fight to keep it there. Which reminds me that I have contracted to give a broadcast talk on W. H. Hudson in a few weeks' time, so, if to-morrow is fine, I will drive over and have a look at this Hampshire village which is now Naboth's vineyard in the eyes of a few misguided folk in Wiltshire.

"You can't farm wi'out muck"

December

Whether there is a scientific explanation of how the human memory works or not I do not know, but until lately I have found it an amazingly efficient tool. Somewhere in man's make-up is a record of every scene and scent and sound with which he has ever come into contact, and by an effort of will it is possible for him to unlock the compartment which contains any one of these, and drag its contents forth for further inspection. Age apparently weakens this power, and I suppose that I must be getting old, for I find that I cannot rely upon my memory with the same certainty of a few years ago. Or is it that this scribbling business of mine makes greater calls upon my memory? Anyway, soon I shall have to keep a notebook, or a diary, or, worse still, get a secretary to keep a record of my daily doings. But a notebook or diary would develop into yet another daily task, while to get a secretary to be nursemaid to my mind would be an admission that I was breaking up. I will do neither. I will try to work into these scribblings for pleasure some of the odds and ends of my life which might otherwise be lost for ever to me, and which may some day come in useful. That last will be the retail milkman coming out in me, I suppose, or else a remnant of my father's dictum, "Check, and double check." Anyway, here goes.

Now what scenes and what conversations of my Norfolk and Scottish trips have left dents in my memory which have not yet been smoothed out by the iron of time and of which I have no record? Norfolk's landscape seemed to be flat and comparatively uninteresting. I should imagine that one rarely needed to change gear in Norfolk. There is no background of hills or mountains, but only farms and hedges and sleepy villages and pheasants and partridges and hares and peasants in continuous repetition everywhere. Also there are muck and sugar-beet and cattle fattening in boxes, each dependent on the other in endless rotation. One farmer told me that " Sugar-beet is all right, but bless 'ee, the partridges don't like 'em. If you want a nice bit of shooting in Norfolk you must grow turnips." Another said : " You can't farm wi'out muck, and you can't get muck wi'out cattle, and in these days you can't get any money to buy cattle unless you grow sugar-beet." I think that I saw the dung cart in use hauling out heaps of muck on to the arable fields more in Norfolk than anywhere I have been in recent years. Another man used a lovely expression to describe this business. " To get a good crop of sugar-beet you want to get your dung carts to work and jam your field all over, good and hearty." Jam, I think, is good.

Some day, if I can work it, I shall try to visit Scotland in the Spring or Summer, when there is more field work going on than there was in November last. So much of the country between Berwick and Edinburgh seems to be governed by the potato that I would like to see the actual operations of planting, and also of the lifting, for during my visit there were only long clamps of stored spuds to be seen. The county of Haddington, I was told, is the one county in Great Britain which has not and never has had a pack of hounds, simply because the lordly potato would not allow such a thing. Another rare thing in that district seemed to be the tractor, for I never saw one at work, all the ploughing being done by Clydesdale horses and mainly by single-furrow ploughs. But what lovely rich land ! It is well worth such care and attention. At some time or other I should imagine that there must have been some French farmers in the south of Scotland, for the harness of the plough teams has a definitely Frenchy appearance. The top of the collar rises up into a kind of single horn, on which the carters hang their overcoats and lunch baskets.

But what a lot of work goes on in the buildings of a Scottish farm during the winter! At one farm I was shown over the steading. I entered by one door, and seemed to walk for miles under the same roof, looking at cattle and pigs and horses, all in covered cattle courts or yards; while, in addition to these, there were barns and sheds innumerable, even the threshing machine being under the same roof. I do not know the extent of this form of farm buildings, and it is difficult to estimate from one walk through in the gloom, but I should imagine that there were at least two acres under one roof. It would be possible, and I expect probable, for a farm labourer—or labouress, for there are a lot of women workers employed—to work for the whole of the winter indoors and never to go out on the farm at all.

Which reminds me of a story I was told about a farmer who never saw his farm for several months during the winter. This occurred before the days of motor transport. The farmer in question had to deliver his milk once daily to Glasgow, a distance which took up the whole day. He used to leave his farm before it was light, and did not get back until after dark, weekdays and Sundays. Fancy a farmer not seeing his farm at all for weeks! How he must have longed for the Spring!

Somehow I have a notion that the sheep farmers in the hills have the better part in Scottish farming, but, like all farmers, even they have their grouses. Their farms are large necessarily, and, in consequence, they are fairly wealthy men, many of whom have been to the university in their youth. From what I could see they all had large houses, well furnished, and fitted with every modern comfort; sheep have never let them down very badly in a financial sense; and many of the younger men ride a hunter worth the thick end of three hundred pounds. "What more do you want?" I asked one of these who was riding a beast which filled me with envy. "Oh, it's all right enough for we men," he replied, "but it's the very devil for our wives. They're stuck up here in the hills with a great big house and scarcely any servants to help them run it, for we can't get maids in the hills. We're too isolated. If a woman doesn't hunt, there's precious little to amuse her up here."

Again I am reminded of a story and of something else which bears on the story. The latter is that in Scotland a dyke is a stone wall, while in Norfolk it is a ditch. The story is the best hunting tale that has come my way since I read *Handley Cross*. But I must remember to stick that down to-morrow, for already it is after midnight, and I have received orders from Charlie, my dairyman, that my services will be required early in the morning.

* * * * * *

In every year there are a few days when outdoor milking will not bear description. Sometimes when it is wet, sometimes when a cold East wind is blowing straight into the bail, and sometimes, what is far more frequent, a thundery afternoon in summer when the fly is busy. Yesterday was one of those days. The almost continuous wet weather of the previous week had turned the lower pastures into a quagmire, and, knowing this, I went up to the bail yesterday afternoon in order to cheer on the sufferers, and to suggest to Charlie that it was high time that we shifted the herd and outfit on to the downs. But conditions were such that Charlie spoke his mind on the subject before I could suggest moving. "Rain er shine we shifts to-morrow," he said. "I bain't gwaine to stay down yer another day fer no man. 'Tis a fair b——." Volumes could not have described the situation more aptly, and I meekly accepted his orders to help in the moving this morning.

And this morning we shifted in pouring rain. This exodus from the low fields every December can best be described by the word "trek," for there is a lot of stuff to shift—engine-house, bail, portable corral, wagon, cart, one bull, and about seventy cows. After much toil and some tribulation, we had the whole outfit happy and comfortable on the clean close turf of the Wiltshire downs, where it will stay until the Spring grass is ready in the water-meadows. Having got wet through in the morning, I made a good job of things by helping to shift the dry cows in the afternoon. Then a bath, a change, and a good tea, and now, as it is still pelting and indoors is much to be preferred to the wet dark outside, is a good chance to put down my Scottish hunting tale on paper. It concerns a charming young lady who married a Border sheep farmer, and, as far as possible, I must try to remember it just as she told it to me. For safety's sake, I will call her Mrs. Armstrong.

" When I came here after our honeymoon," she said, " I soon discovered that unless you took an interest in sheep or hunting you might just as well be dead, for that's all there is on the Border, Mr. Street—just sheep and hunting. Of course, I knew nothing about either, so as hunting is the more important, Bill there bought me a horse and began teaching me to ride. But when the first meet came along the dirty dog told me that I couldn't ride up to Border standard, and therefore that I could not go hunting with him. You can do anything with these Border men, but you mustn't let them down in front of their friends. When I inquired meekly what I was supposed to do all day while he was enjoying himself, he said, ' You can go to the meet in the car, and take Whitey with you. She's the best terrier on the Border. Often the fox goes to ground. After

Who in hell let out that bl..dy terrier?

the meet you drive on to the top of the hills, and if you see the hunt stopped anywhere, drive up with Whitey and you'll be very welcome.' So, of course, I obeyed.

" Well, I went to the meet, where I was introduced to various people on horseback as the blushing English bride. Then, when they had all moved off, I drove up to the top of a hill, where I stopped the car and smoked a cigarette. Then I think I must have dropped to sleep, for when I woke up it was to see a fox trotting across the road only a little way from the car.

" I'd never seen a fox before, so when he crept through a gap in a dyke near by, I got out of the car and crept quietly towards the dyke in order to see where he had gone. I peeped over the dyke, and there was Mr. Fox sunning himself on the far side. Then I thought to myself, 'There's all those people and horses and hounds trying to catch a fox. I wonder if Whitey can catch this one. If she can, all those hunting people will be awfully pleased with me.' So I crept back to the car, took Whitey in my arms, crept on tiptoe back to the dyke, lifted her up, and dropped her right on top of the fox, saying: 'Good dog, Whitey! Seize him!'

"And she did! She did! She gripped him and hung on. And there was I leaning over the dyke, listening to the most awful row, wondering what would happen next, and thinking how grateful everybody would be to me for catching their fox, and how proud and pleased my husband would be."

At this point I yelped my delight aloud, while her husband grinned his appreciation of the joke. "What happened next?" I asked.

"Heaps of things. In a minute or two I saw the hounds tearing along the hillside towards me, with several horsemen galloping along behind them, so I ran back to the car to be out of the way. The hounds came up and made an awful row as they set into my fox. Then up came the Master and two or three more. They sat on their horses and watched the business, and the Master bellowed: 'Who in the hell let out that bloody terrier?' And then, would you believe it? That husband of mine, who was next to him, shouted: 'I don't know, Master. I've never seen the damn dog before.' And it was his own terrier, the dirty liar."

I shouted with laughter at this, while her husband grinned steadily. He was a good grinner, that man. "And then?" I queried, for it seemed to me that there must be more to follow.

"Then? Oh, the Border experts finished the business, and presently they all rode off. Not one of them had the decency to thank me for catching their fox. In fact, none of them came near me. At least, only Bill. He waited until they were all gone, and then rode up to the car with Whitey in his arms. He was white with rage. He tossed her into the back of the car, and said : 'Prue ! Cover that dog up with a rug and go straight home.' The pig, and me only married a bare three months ! "

" And so ended your first day's hunting, Mrs. Armstrong," I remarked. " But I have heard on good authority that now you are in the first flight with hounds, and that the Master eats out of your hand. How did these Border experts educate you so efficiently ? "

" By chaff mostly, Mr. Street. They're pets really, most of 'em, but they're devils at leg-pulling. Why, that same night Bill brought the Master in for a drink. He never said a word about Whitey's exploit while he was indoors, so I thought that he didn't know I was responsible. I gave him a dram and he was charming. But when he got up to go, he thanked me for entertaining him, and then, just as he was disappearing through the door, he said : 'Whitey's a jolly good terrier, isn't she, Mrs. Armstrong ? And how well you manage her.' And he was gone before I could get in one word, and afterwards the dirty blighter spread the tale all through the Border, so that wherever I went people complimented me on my handling of terriers. Still, he's been awfully kind to me since."

Such, I imagine, is the method of a Border education !

* * * * * *

Bad times during recent years have caused many farmers to give up shooting and to let their sporting rights, thus taking a little money and saving the expenditure for game certificate and cartridges. I had my first game certificate twenty years ago, and held one continuously every year until 1927, when, for financial reasons, this pleasant luxury had to be given up. Since that date, in common with many of my farmer neighbours, I have only taken my gun down from the wall in order to kill vermin or to bag a dinner, and, quite frankly, I have envied the financial status of various shooting tenants in the neighbourhood.

However, the other day one of my neighbours, a very good friend, invited me to go shooting. Apparently the shooting tenant having given up the shooting of his farm, he was keeping it himself—at any rate, for one year. Whether this can be taken as a sign that farming has turned the corner I cannot say, but it did recall to me the pleasures of days gone by. Even so, I hesitated to accept. I was woefully out of practice, and feared that I should make a mess of things. It seemed better to refuse gracefully and regretfully, and so retain intact the glory of my past reputation.

But my friend would have none of it. "You've got to come," he said. "We shan't get much, but we shall have some fun, and 'twill be like old times to have you, and Walter, and Jim, shooting with me on my place once again. We'm getting older now, but there'll be my boys to walk with the beaters like we used to do. Don't tell me you can't shoot. We'll show the youngsters a thing or two, and I won't take 'No' for an answer. You've got to come along." Usually when people say that I *must* do something, I stick my toes in firmly and refuse, but when a farmer friend of old standing says so, there is nothing for it but to obey; so I gave way and spent some time yesterday evening in cleaning up my gun.

To-day then at 10 a.m. I found myself walking along a track through a large wood in company with my host and five or six friends. His sons and beaters were approaching the wood by another route in order to drive in any birds which might be out in the fields. When we reached the boundary the plan of campaign was carried out in the form of a letter L; the beaters being the long upright stroke, the guests the short horizontal one, while the little tail to the rear of the junction of these was represented by our host, according to ancient custom. "And keep your eyes open for deer," was his final injunction. Then with shouts and clatter the beaters started, and I dawdled along the ride ahead of them, keeping my proper distance from the gun on either side of me.

And once again I was conscious, not only that shooting was a pleasurable thing, but also that it was a natural part of a farming life. Overhead the pale December sun shone in a limpid blue sky. The trees around were bare, but the undergrowth was a thick mass of bracken and brambles, for, as in most large woods, clearing this is a job which, perforce, has been neglected for many seasons. I listened to the beaters enjoying themselves. " Hi, hi, hi ! " they shouted. Then suddenly : " Woodcock over on the right." Then " Over back ! " came a yell from one of them, and I turned to watch our host take him neatly, first barrel, again according to ancient custom. " Forrad on. Ee'm all right, you. The Guvner done 'is little bit o' business proper."

History seemed suddenly to have gone back twenty-odd years, and here was I taking part in it. Forgotten were business cares and every worry connected with the world which existed outside this patch of brown December woodland. The only worries I possessed were, firstly, would anything come my way? and secondly, should I disgrace myself if it did ? Besides, just supposing there was a deer ! Here and there a pheasant got up. Some were accounted for by my host's sons, who were struggling through the dense undergrowth along with the beaters. Others whirled away over the line of guns, some falling, and others escaping unhurt into the security of the woods below, but as yet none had come near enough to test my skill.

Then suddenly there was a yell : " Pheasant over on the right ! " and I could see a cock coming fast in a nasty swerve which would bring him straight over me. He came so quickly that I had no time either to aim or to think. My gun went up,

"Deer up" they yelled.

swung naturally, and without my being conscious of pulling the trigger I saw the bird crumple up and fall in a glorious curve. " And that's all right," I muttered, as I reloaded quickly. " A good start's half the battle."

This proved to be correct. Had I missed that first bird most probably I should have continued to miss them, spending most of the day in search of the correct formula of hand and eye and swing, but as it was, I do not remember ever shooting better than I did that morning.

Then suddenly there was pandemonium amongst the beaters. "Deer up! Deer up!" they yelled. I peered eagerly into the undergrowth before me, but could see nothing. Then I heard much talk and laughter, and I could see that the line of beaters had halted. " What's up ? " yelled our host, and half a dozen voices gave reply. " On'y Shiner bin a vell awver a deer. Trod right on un. 'Ee's gone back. Pick theeself up, Shiner. I low the bist a zight more vrightened than 'ee. Forrad on."

Then my host had not been leg-pulling. There were some wild deer in the wood. I decided to keep my eyes well open for them. Presently, during a short halt while a bird was being picked up, I fancied I saw a movement in the bracken. I watched carefully, and caught a momentary glimpse of a deer's head. When the beaters started again there appeared to be a disturbance in the undergrowth coming towards me. I waited, with itching finger. Two shots in rapid succession to the rear caused whatever was moving there to rush quickly forward, and then, within twenty yards' range, I caught a glimpse of a deer running between two clumps of hazel. It was safe to shoot as he was well ahead of the beaters, and I had the satisfaction of seeing him go head-over-heels to my first barrel.

I was next to our host, so I called to him that I had bagged a deer. He ordered the beaters to halt, and together we pushed our way through the bracken. Just as we arrived where we could see the deer lying dead his golden retriever rushed forward and tried to retrieve the animal just as though it had been a hare. Never have I seen anything quite so comic. He is a dear dog, but an awful fool, and, most probably, he would have done just the same if it had been a tiger lying there. We hauled the deer out on to the ride, hung it up to a tree, and then moved on, everybody keeping a sharp look-out for more deer.

And so the golden December day went on. It was not a swell shoot. The guns were farmers, and the beaters were, with the exception of a retired policeman who joined in the fun, farm labourers. We lunched simply in a sunny, squelchy ride, during which we talked farming and chaffed each other unmercifully. The bag broke no records, consisting of but twenty-odd pheasants, a few hares and rabbits, two jays, three woodcock, one pigeon and two deer, for we got another of these after lunch. At dusk we piled into the lorry which usually is filled with milk churns, and returned to the farmhouse, where, tired and happy, we did justice to a most excellent tea.

Such is a farmer's day, and in this particular one three things stand out in my mind. Firstly, a personal satisfaction that I have not forgotten how to shoot moderately decently; secondly, that wild deer have greatly increased during recent years; and thirdly, that for country folk to shoot their own countryside is right somehow. Some people will perhaps call us barbarians and clods for taking our pleasures in this fashion, but I, for one, will not mind, for in doing so they will tell me that their criticism is valueless, simply because they themselves have never participated in a farmer's day.

* * * * * *

A wet green Christmas Day. On several occasions I have been asked to write an article dealing with Christmas in the country, and always I have refused, saying that in these days there are no great festivities at Christmas in rural districts, beyond the ordinary family ones which occur in every household in the land, both town and country. I can dimly remember some local mummers acting a play in this house when I was a very small boy, but now Christmas comes and goes each year without any special happenings, much like any other general holiday. Country folk, according to their inclinations and financial abilities, amuse themselves during the leisure which this season brings in much the same fashion as they do on their weekly half-day; which, although it may sound unromantic and rather dull, is a true statement of the case.

However, this afternoon I managed to do something which I have never before done on Christmas Day. It was too wet for golf, too wet for shooting—too wet for anything sensible, according to my wife—so I did something which she called foolish. I went fishing on a lake with my brother-in-law—also a fool like myself, to quote his better half—and his small boy, who has not yet attained years of discretion.

We drove ten miles by car before we arrived at the scene of foolery, and then, arrayed in mackintoshes, we rowed a heavy punt into the middle of the lake and fished for perch. Really the rain was such that we warranted our wives' description, but we stuck it out long enough to catch a dozen perch, and so were able to confound the ladies with this success on our return. Then, wet through but extraordinarily cheerful, we retired to the bathroom and turned on the hot tap. Somehow or other it occurs to me that rarely have I enjoyed a Christmas afternoon quite so well, or faced a turkey in the evening half so manfully.

* * * * * *

Whilst I was up on the downs this morning I could not help thinking that no lover of the countryside should scorn December in Downland. Now the countryside is at rest, sleeping her long Winter sleep in order to wake refreshed at the call of Spring; and while she sleeps one can study her more closely. Why? Simply because Nature's way in fashion is exactly opposite to that of mankind. In the Summer she wears her heaviest clothing, while in Winter she goes naked—in truth, a brave lady for whom I have a profound respect.

This morning, although much of the life and colour which made the Summer scene so glorious was missing, I discovered that by reason of Nature's nakedness I could see much more detail of the countryside. Lanes and fields—even my own fields which I have known since babyhood—seemed suddenly to have become strangers, and as the day was warm I lingered for awhile on the downs in order to renew their acquaintance. My oldest friends amongst the trees in the valley had altered out of all recognition, for when I last gazed on this scene they were garbed in Autumn's flaming beauty. To-day they seemed rather forbidding, but after studying them for a few moments I found a curious beauty in their bare skeletons, and knew them once again for true friends who are lovely at every season. Soon, I thought, in January most likely, the frost will take pity on their nakedness and clothe their gaunt frames with silver lace.

In one place in the downs there is an old Roman road which runs straight as a bowstring towards Old Sarum. Down in the valley below it disappears, for there the plough, that all-conquering implement, held sway for centuries until I grassed that field down some five or six years ago; but this morning it was clear enough for me to pick up the road on the far hillside, a full mile away. Whilst looking at this, I noticed something which I had never spotted before—that many of the field gates, even in the ploughed fields, are placed exactly in its line. This evening I took the trouble to check this fact on an old hunting map, and found that wherever possible the country folk of these parts have set their gates and placed their gaps on the line of the old Roman road.

It is curious how clear the air is sometimes at this season, and also how much better sound carries in Winter than it does in Summer. This morning I could see almost minute details of the farming operations which were taking place on the hillside across the Wylye valley ; while the tinkle of sheepbells there was so loud and clear that it did not seem possible that the sheep which carried them could be more than a mile away. Carts laden with manure, hauled by three horses at length, were crawling slowly, oh so slowly, from the dung-yards uphill towards a field where the carter was putting out the manure in heaps, each heap and each row of heaps set the requisite number of paces apart. On one side of the field two men were busy spreading the manure, and I could see the lift and thrust of their forks at every stroke.

Higher up the hillside the shepherd was pitching his fold for to-morrow, and I watched the black line of the hurdles grow longer as he worked, and even made out his dog pottering about near by. Lower down the hill a herd of cows was spread out in horseshoe formation, busily eating hay which had been dropped from a wagon in this design; while lower still I could see my own drowner at work in the meadows cleaning out the irrigation ditches, the flash of his sharp tool showing brightly in the sunlight at regular intervals. Preparation, preparation, and still more preparation for things to come, that is the business of farming, I thought, a business which never stops from January to December.

* * * * * *

In one hour from now the bells will ring in the New Year, so this should be a fitting time to think a little about the Old

Year and make plans and possibly resolutions for the New. Youth should look, must look forward ; old age must, perforce, look back ; but surely middle-age such as mine should look both ways on the lines of " That was you, you fool, that was. And now, what are you going to do ? "

But to set my foolish actions of a year down on paper would be merely rubbing it in—and, anyway, I've paid for them ; while to put down an account of the rare occasions on which I exhibited a little wisdom or a faint streak of decency would savour of conceit. To generalise will be best. From a farming point of view I can say truthfully that, while farming has not bettered itself very much, if at all, during the year, a note of hope has crept into it. Our statesmen have done all sorts of things with the idea of improving its position with little success, but by means of trial and error I presume that some day they will find the right solution. Anyway, they have achieved one worth-while thing—they have managed to make the nation " agriculture conscious " ; which was how an enthusiastic American gentleman described to me the effect on the audience which he required from a film dealing with country life.

But films are beyond me. Still, I must not grumble. Rather should I give thanks to the past year for the continuance of my good fortune in the book world. This is so amazing that again and again I find myself wondering whether it is not all a dream ; but a glance at my bookshelf tells me that it is true, and once again reminds me to be grateful for such good luck.

For good luck it was for me when I stumbled into this writing game. Three years before an almost bankrupt farmer ; then a hard-working producer-retailer of milk, struggling slowly but surely on to firmer financial ground ; and then, suddenly, an author. How well I remember when my first book was published ! Prior to its publication only a few local friends knew of its coming, and for weeks I had done my delivery rounds by day and my milk books during the evenings, metaphorically hugging myself at the thought of publication day, which was coming nearer and nearer. Then, a few days before this great day, six copies of my book arrived, telling me for certain that the dream was no dream but a reality ; and then on a Thursday the reality arrived.

Still I held myself in, for my farming life had long taught me not to tell of success but to let such news come to my neighbours from outside sources, thereby gaining greatly in value. Besides, although my book was published, it was too early to say whether it was a success or a failure. On Thursday there was one fairly favourable review ; Friday and Saturday each brought another ; so on Saturday night I decided to cut loose on the Sunday. To-day the fashion of that celebration seems rather childish although very understandable, but even now I can appreciate how suited it was to the occasion. Wine, feasting, music, and all the customary things in which man indulges when he rejoices, I ignored. These might satisfy ordinary folk, but a farmer-milkman who had just published his first book must jubilate in more subtle fashion.

For several years I had risen both weekdays and Sundays at 4.30 a.m. in order to pursue my calling as a farmer-milkman. But now, I thought, come what may, I am a blooming author. Authors do not get up at such an unearthly hour. Authors rise late. Authors have been known to breakfast in bed. To-morrow then, I, a farmer-milkman, will have my breakfast in bed. Accordingly I arranged to pay a man to do my usual Sunday morning work ; I instructed my Salisbury roundsman to bring back half a dozen Sunday newspapers ; and I banished the alarum clock from my bedroom.

Sunday morning arrived, and while my wife and I were

breakfasting in luxury for once we heard the Salisbury milk van return home, just before nine o'clock. In a few minutes the papers arrived, and in one of them we found a full-page review of my book. And then, half-way between laughter and tears, midst a welter of newspapers and breakfast things, we hugged each other like two small children.

Since that wonderful moment I have continued writing with some success, and surely therefore I should be grateful for this good fortune, not only for its material side, but also for the joy which goes with it. For to write a book which is not an absolute flop must bring great joy to any man or woman, especially if the first book be written in middle-age. Or so it always seems to me; and particularly at this moment when the Old Year is dying and a New Year is about to be born. Some day I shall die, but here is my secret pride. Years after I am dead, someone will buy a bundle of books for a few shillings at an auction sale, and amongst them find and read one of mine. Then, although I shall be lying safe in Wiltshire's chalk, I shall live again in the reader's mind for an hour or two. That, in itself, takes away much of my natural fear of death. " What a fool! " many folks would say, but while I live no one can take this foolish comfort from me. So for this year and for every year I have lived in order to attain this year, I give grateful thanks.

Hark! There are the bells. The Old Year is dead and the New Year is born. Sleep well, old friend, for I am greatly in your debt. You died, naked and unashamed, a strong old man at the end of a useful life. May I copy your example when my time comes!

To your successor I wish good fortune, but I will make him only one resolution, and that is that I will try to be a little more grateful in the future for the luck which the past has brought me.

January

The Old Year went out in floods of tears, the New Year came in warm and wet, and for some days now all my non-farming friends and acquaintances have been cursing the weather. They told me that it was muggy, unhealthy, bad for trade, unseasonable, that we should suffer for it, and again and again they yearned loud and long for cold, seasonable frost; which, they told me, would brace everybody up. Silly asses! I do not want to be braced up, not one little bit. I am a farmer, and I know that frost has a nasty habit of costing me money for extra food for my animals, especially for my cows, and that even with this extra expense their milk yield goes steadily down. Give me warm, wet weather every time in preference, for I agree with the old saying, " More rain, more grass; more butter, more brass."

However, before the year was ten days old my friends got their wish, and to-day and yesterday have been cold and frosty, with every promise of still colder weather to follow. For several days there has been fog, and yesterday we did not see the sun at all, save for a moment at sundown when he flamed angrily in omen of the morrow's frost. To-day there is no fog, but the sky is a dull leaden grey, and the world seems dead. Nothing moves. There is not enough wind even to ruffle the gaunt skeletons of the trees, and the tall poplars in the meadows stand motionless like sentinels. The downs seem to frown gloomily on to the valley beneath, and there is not one smile in all the landscape. Winter, cold, unfriendly Winter, reigns supreme in sombre, silent dignity.

Somehow I find it difficult to love Winter, for, although he be a just monarch, he rarely tempers his justice with mercy. Still, perhaps he is wise. Were he to withhold just punishment from the unthinking, the inefficient, and the foolish, neither man, bird, nor beast, would respect him. Civilisation may try to run the world in this fashion, but Winter rules each year for a space without mercy—cold, and still, and silent, and just.

Consequently those foolish ones, who refuse or forget to look upon his annual dominion as one of those things which must inevitably be, are doomed to suffer. For instance, on Christmas Day there was a blackbird sitting on four eggs in a nest in the laurels at the bottom of the lawn. To-day that nest is deserted and the eggs are cold. Justice for fools possibly, but somehow I wish that Winter were a trifle more merciful.

But wishing is no good. Every year Winter rules the countryside for awhile in dictatorial fashion. Nowadays dictators are many and various, but never was there such a stern dictator as Winter, nor so stringent a decree as his decree of frost. Under its rule the hunt rides no more, the plough lies useless on the headland, the wind is stilled, and even the rivers cease their flow. Which reminds me that my small daughter does not agree with her father over this question of frost. She is yearning for more and more frost so that there will be skating, whilst I am hoping against hope that she will be disappointed.

Still, if the frost does hold we may as well try to get some fun out of it, for rural skating has its points. Do not talk to me of indoor rinks, with their waltzing and their figure skating and their perfect surfaces. To obtain the full enjoyment from skating you must skate on a village meadow, which some wily farmer, smelling the coming frost, has flooded in readiness : for when this happens you will find every grade of rural society pleasuring on the ice.

Old and young, rich and poor, the butcher, the baker, the

poacher, the keeper, landlord and tenant, church and chapel, tory and socialist, men, women and children ; everybody in the district comes to the meadow when the news goes round that the ice bears. Now is the chance for old age to show youth a thing or two, and those who learned to skate fifty years ago seize it gratefully ; many a grandfather and even a grandmother astonishing their usually scornful descendants with their graceful prowess. It is useless for the young experts who have learnt their skating indoors to grumble either at the roughness of the ice or at the many sliding children who get in their way so often. This is the one revel of movement which King Winter permits his country subjects—let us enjoy it while we can and be thankful.

Sixpence for adults and threepence for children is the charge. Cars and bicycles line the lane, and skates of all patterns and ages are used, the very latest on the feet of the under thirties, and the very ancient types on those feet whose owners are well over fifty; for, curiously enough, few middle-aged country folk seem to be able to skate. In their youth there were few hard winters, and nowadays they are too shy to learn skating indoors, exposed to the critical gaze of modern youth. Of such am I, and maybe that is another reason for my dislike of frost.

Even so, I always attend this local skating when it takes place, for the surprises to be seen are numerous. Here is old General So-and-So, a peppery, forbidding person usually, gliding along, beaming at everybody. And there is Mrs. Somebody-Else, a recognised invalid who is rarely seen out of doors during the Winter—just look how gracefully she moves on those old-fashioned skates. But who is this ? The postman, our old fat postman whom we have seen hobbling along the roads all the Summer. Just look at him ! He is in uniform with an ancient pair of skates partly strapped and partly tied to his boots with string. And can't he skate ! Why, he's an expert !

The last time I met him on the ice I asked him where he learnt to skate, and he told me that in his youth he had skated up the river for miles. How I hope that he will not be able to do that this year!

One thing which always strikes me very forcibly when I visit the scene of our local skating is the general air of friendliness to be found there. On the ice old quarrels are forgotten, and class distinctions do not exist. When sides are picked for a game of hockey, both the General and the Rector are eager to bag the postman, whose round, red face is one glorious sunset of happiness at the unaccustomed friendliness and exercise. And there goes the policeman—flat on his back! Verily, ice in a country meadow is a great leveller in more ways than one.

But this year I, who cannot skate and who have a farm under my care, hope that there will be no skating, and that Winter will soon rescind his decree of frost. His rain and his winds I do not mind, for I know the former to be a boon and the latter merely bluster. But before his frost and its accompanying awful hush, I cower most humbly, which is bad for my self-respect, and incidentally for my pocket also.

* * * * * *

Winter is on my side this season, for the frost turned to rain long before my skating friends could get busy, and to-day there is almost a hint of Spring in the air—enough, anyway, to make me think about the coming hay-crop. To-day I have been walking round my pastures trying to make up my mind which of these to dress with artificial manure and what type of dressing to use. The manurial residue of the cake fed to the dairy herd is having a steady and continuous beneficial effect, but those fields which are to be cut for hay will pay for a dose of fertiliser.

One of the great difficulties about this business is how to apply the manure. Men who can sow manure moderately evenly by hand are very scarce nowadays, and, anyway, it is a rotten job to ask any man to do. I can remember seeing my father's labourers with their eyes bunged up with soot after sowing this manure by hand on a windy day ; and there are few artificial manures to-day which do not cause similar discomfort and ruined clothing to the hand sower.

Therefore, a mechanical manure distributor is needed, and I do not possess one. I have had several in my time, but up to date have never possessed a satisfactory one, and now my farm is too small to warrant the necessary capital expenditure. I want to run over about a hundred acres—say a good week's work for a distributor. The work will not wear it out, but the deterioration which will take place while the machine is idle will do so. Many farmers must experience the same difficulty, and I am sure that were manure manufacturers to offer to sell their products *spread*, their sales would more than double. In these days of motor transport to do this for an adequate charge per ton should not be impossible. Anyway, I, in common with many other small farmers, shall not buy any artificials until I can find a way to get them spread without going to the expense of buying a distributor. It occurs to me that our inventors might well try to invent a better type of machine for this job and also a much cheaper one.

* * * * * *

Already there are newly-born lambs on the hillsides, and this morning I paid a visit to a neighbour's lambing-pen. I gave up keeping a lambing flock a dozen years ago, but the sight of this one brought back many memories of my shepherding days : especially when the shepherd, in answer to my tactful inquiry, said : " We've 'ad vairish luck thease roun'." How well I remember the lambing pens of my youth and the good and bad

Hedger at work

luck which attended them! One lambing season when I was about seventeen I had the misfortune, or perhaps the good fortune, to be the connecting link between a gloomy shepherd, whose flock was in the throes of bad luck, and a Victorian father who was in bed with rheumatism. How I suffered, but what a lot of farming knowledge I acquired in the process!

However, local gossip tells me that lambing luck generally is good this season, and this morning I watched the shepherd carry in three pairs of twins as against two singles dropped during my visit. And this reminded me that personally I owe a great debt of gratitude to a Wiltshire shepherd who, in my youth, initiated me so finely into the mysteries of both birth and death. Never shall I forget the thrill I experienced in my teens, when, for the first time in my life, I picked up in my hands a twin of lambs but a few moments old and carried them into shelter.

That little scene in the theatre of my life began with but two actors—an inexperienced, rather frightened boy, and a Hampshire Down ewe. A few minutes later four actors were playing their parts perfectly, and three of them without benefit of rehearsal. Somehow I do not think that it is possible for any lad to be introduced to the beginning of life in finer fashion.

To-day's visit to that sheep-fold pleased me greatly, for the other day I saw a machine for trimming hedges ; which means, I suppose, that soon another old-time craftsman, the hedger in his apron of sacking, will be superseded by the machine and the overalled mechanic. It is dangerous to prophesy, I know, but I do not think anyone in my lifetime will invent a machine which will lamb down a flock of ewes satisfactorily. So my friends the shepherds are safe, even if all other farming is to be a business of knives and cog-wheels. Again I think of the manure distributor, and suggest to our inventors that they would have been better advised to leave the hedging to the hedger, while they devoted their attention to producing an efficient and cheap machine for distributing artificial manures, a machine which farming really does need. However, I have solved my distributing problem for this year by arranging with a neighbour to come down with a distributor and an old car to haul it, and spread my manures at a fair charge.

* * * * * *

Although the frost has gone, Winter continues to give us a taste of his quality. For several days now the countryside has been inhabited and dominated by a cold, very cold, wind, and to-day, presumably because I had arranged to go shooting, the wind was rougher and colder than ever. There is usually a stiffish breeze on the top of the hills on the east side of the Avon valley above Netheravon, and to-day there was a howling gale, which saved the lives of several partridges as far as I was concerned. With the wind under their tails they came straight at me, and for the first two drives went straight past me, unscathed.

Possibly there was some excuse, for I had not met the driven partridge for seven or eight years until this morning, when he cut me dead. However, the obvious reason for my failure was that I was shooting behind them, so after each failure I increased the margin, but for some time with no result. Finally, in desperation and shame, I swung a full twenty yards it seemed in front of the leader of a covey, pulled the trigger, and had the satisfaction of seeing him shut up on the instant. Without slowing down the swing of my gun, I shifted on to the rear bird of all, and he did likewise. The latter was a fluke, but it appeared so workmanlike that I did not confess it as such to my friends. Very reprehensible this conduct, I suppose, but I daresay they were just as guilty as I.

Nowadays in this spacious Wiltshire country the ubiquitous motor-car is a great help in January partridge shooting, when the party has to cover a lot of ground in the day. In spite of ruts, mud, and no semblance of road, it is possible to get about on the hills in a car, if you are accustomed to his mode of cross-country travel. To-day most farmers are experts at this, for few of them ride or drive a horse, and their car has to transport them over country which even the most enthusiastic motor-car salesman would think impossible.

But although the average farmer is and has to be a good car driver, he has one great fault—he will take more interest in the countryside on either side of the road than on the road itself. This is understandable, I suppose, for farming is his ruling passion ; but it can be very risky, and sometimes amusing. I can remember a farming neighbour, a man who uses a car most shamefully and who always drives over any country like Jehu, son of Nimshi, driving me back from Brighton to Salisbury on a summer afternoon. Forgetting that he was not in his native Wiltshire and that the road was crowded with traffic, he criticised the farming of Sussex as we journeyed. Seeing a motor-car hay-sweep at work over the hedge, without any warning he pulled up suddenly in order to watch its progress, whereupon a small sports car nearly ran into us from behind. Its driver, a most charming young lady, managed to save a smash, but as she drove slowly past us she yelled at my friend: "You bloody fool! You ought to be pushing a pram." Whereupon my friend took off his hat with a flourish and replied: "Madam, I apologise. You are quite right. But so ought you!" Whereupon the girl laughed gaily, put her foot on the accelerator, and streaked off down the road. Honours, I think, were easy.

* * * * * *

I have agreed to let a friend's son come up to this farm by day for about six months as a sort of farm pupil. I have given up taking pupils for some time, because now that I am away from home so much I am not the right type of farmer to teach a lad. A boy should go to a man whose sole means of livelihood is his farm, and also he should live with such a farmer in the farm-house, as then, and only then, will he learn that farming never stops, and that his pleasure and leisure must come second to the farm's needs.

But this case was exceptional. The lad's father lives within a quarter-mile, and the lad, who has just left school, has to put in six months on a farm in order to qualify him to go to college in September. He is an attractive youth, but how young he is—or, rather, how old he makes me feel! And yet, looking at a photograph of myself taken when I was eighteen tells me that I was even more immature at that age. But the day after that snapshot was taken I was on a liner bound for Canada, and the life there soon ripened me to manhood. Well, this lad will get old fast enough. I turned out one pupil a successful farmer after but six months on this farm, and to-day, even if I cannot give this lad such intensive training, I must do what I can. His is the right age to start. "If you don't buy colts, you've never got 'osses."

Which reminds me that he is mad keen on horses, and is rather disappointed that we have only one horse on this three-hundred-odd acres, and that a fat old carthorse which lives out of doors Winter and Summer. I shall have to point out to him that in farming to-day horses play a rapidly diminishing part, and that if a farmer wants to keep hunters for pleasure, he must first make his farm pay in order to afford the luxury. That is, of course, just the sort of thing my father used to tell me, and also the sort of thing I never thought I should want to say to anyone. It just shows how old I am getting.

*   *   *   *   *   *

My wife has been worrying me about the state of the garden. Like most farmers I am a bad gardener, and with regard to my own garden I am, therefore, the despair of my wife. Of course, I like the produce of a garden. Who does not? Why, even to enumerate some of the delicacies which our garden provides for me every year in spite of my persistent neglect almost makes my mouth water. Young spring onions, crunchy hearts of lettuce, asparagus, green peas—ah, why continue such a row of tantalus? Rather let me say: "Hurry on, Spring, and let Summer follow you quickly."

But to return to the farmhouse garden and my shameful neglect of it. In this I am only carrying on the tradition of my forefathers. For as far back as I can remember this garden was tended by that most unfortunate of all farm employees, a groom-gardener. This man had to be a veritable jack-of-all-trades, and,

The Groom Gardener

naturally enough, as my father paid his wages, he saw to it that my father's wishes came first, and the garden a bad, very bad, second. In the old days he had three nags to look after; he milked six cows night and morning; he took the milk to the station; he cleaned the boots; he got in the coals and wood; he helped on the farm when required; and, as my father was crippled with rheumatism, at any hour of the day a yell from an open window meant that the pony and trap must arrive on the drive in a few moments. Fortunately for my mother and the garden, this farm is on the chalk, and therefore the groom-gardener was permitted to spend his spare time in the garden; for, had it been on clay, I feel sure that all the groom-gardeners of my youth would have been engaged during their leisure hours in brick-making.

Somehow I do not think that the duties of groom and of gardener can ever be performed satisfactorily by one individual. If he be a good groom, then most probably he will be a bad gardener. Conversely, if he be a good gardener, who possesses both green fingers and the gardener's thumb, then, for certain, he will be an untidy, slovenly groom; and, as such, an employee which no self-respecting farmer who keeps horses can tolerate. That, I think, is the real reason why so many farmers' gardens show signs of neglect.

Of course, during my farming days the coming of the car drove the nag horse away from the farm, but this happening did not lighten the groom-gardener's duties one little bit. Someone had to drive the milk lorry, and who so fitted for this duty as the groom-gardener, who to-day should be called the chauffeur-gardener? Again I experienced the same difficulty of finding a man who could and would perform a dual rôle satisfactorily, but once I did find such a man, truly a pearl of great value. What I did with him is a shameful confession to make, but truth must be told—he was much too good a man to waste in the garden, and so I made him foreman over seven hundred acres, a post which he filled most admirably.

Then, some years later, came a time when my farming could no longer pay for the services of either groom-gardener or chauffeur-gardener, and the only man who could be spared for occasional gardening was the " drowner," a craftsman of high degree. His first and only love was his water-meadows, and he would only go gardening as a special favour. Indeed, according to my wife, he used to invent excuses to return to his meadows, for I can remember her saying to me : " You said that I could have Jim in the garden for a week. He stayed two days, and this morning he told me that he must do something down the meadows. And he's gone off. If he were a younger man, I should think he met his best girl down there." I must say that it seemed like it.

But to-day I am well served both in gardening and all sorts of other things by one man, an amazing fellow who manages to keep cheerful in spite of his manifold duties. Even so, just now, when Spring is imminent, I, a non-gardener, can see that the garden requires more of his time than he can possibly give it ; and so I have ordained that Jim, that same " drowner," shall spend a full week there. His meadow work is over for awhile, and therefore he can have no objection to doing a little gardening, while, as a result, I shall go up a trifle in my wife's estimation—a step which is long overdue.

However, in spite of my and other farmers' neglect of our gardens, it is amazing what a lot of good stuff they produce, which speaks well for that much-maligned, hard-working body of men called groom-gardeners, chauffeur-gardeners, handymen, or what you will. For the toothsome dainties they provide and their cheerfulness while bearing almost superhuman burdens

Hampshire must be the rabbits' spiritual home.

I take off my hat to all such men, for in both these matters they are better men than I. It may be that this respect is due to the fact that recently I have found myself taking an increasing interest in the garden. Sometimes I try to persuade myself that this is because increasing years are curtailing my participation in more active pursuits ; but I know that this is not the real reason, which is that no longer am I wholly a farmer. A hybrid being such as I have become, half-writer and half-farmer, may well take to gardening in his leisure hours ; but a true farmer will never do so. Wives of farmers will say that this is a pity, but also they must add : " And pity 'tis, 'tis true."

*   *   *   *   *   *

All my life I have looked upon Hampshire as being an inferior county to Wiltshire with regard to farming. This is partly due to a Wiltshireman's natural preference for his native county, but chiefly because such a lot of Hampshire land is a thin, light gravel which peters out in a drought much more quickly than our Wiltshire chalk. But to-day that dividing line between the Southern and Mid-Western Regions fixed by the Milk Marketing Board makes Hampshire farms much more desirable. In consequence, two of my Wiltshire farming friends are hunting a farm in Hants, and this morning I went with them to spy out the land.

Apparently they had the offer of two farms. One, according to the agent in charge of the business, was a good one which he reckoned he could let without much difficulty ; while the other was a barren, poor place which just had to be let somehow. Armed with a map and full particulars we set off, deciding to explore the worst farm first. We drove miles over downs and poor pastures which appeared to be stocked almost solely by rabbits. Hampshire is the rabbit's spiritual home. Rabbits innumerable, rabbits in the hedgerows, rabbits in burrows on the open down, and rabbits sitting in the sun, who did not move until our car was almost on top of them. A poor, barren farm peopled by rabbits, but it had a water supply, it was accessible, it lay nicely to the sun—in short, it had possibilities. Or so I thought, but I did not voice this opinion to my companions, for they were two of the most hard-bitten farmers in the South-west. Accordingly I opened gates innumerable for them, and listened to their remarks in silence as befitted a comparative novice. Having bumped over nearly every acre of this farm they decided to try the better one. " Dam' poor and lousy with rabbits," said the one who was driving. " Let's go and see what So-and-So calls a desirable farm."

A quarter of an hour's run brought us to it, and then my gate-opening capabilities were tested once more, while we motored over the desirable farm. Again rabbits innumerable, but this time rabbits in nasty, ugly belts of overgrown hedgerow at least thirty yards wide. Also a lot of nasty, sour, hilly arable land. Also a rutty farm road with a stiff gradient, so rutty and muddy that our car got stuck going downhill, and only by good luck and some strenuous pushing by two of us assisted by three carters who were ploughing near by did we get going again. Then, down in the valley some water-meadows which had been let go to such an extent that they were a dense mat of rushes—in my opinion a liability rather than an asset, and certainly not desirable.

Having looked at every field my crafty companions asked me what I thought about this farm. Not by word or gesture had they given me any idea of their own opinion, so I had to risk my reputation on my own judgment. There was no dodging it, so I took my courage in both hands and said : " I'd sooner have the poor farm." " And so'd I," said our chauffeur, " and so'd anybody with an ounce of common sense. Old So-and-So may call this bitch of a place a desirable farm, but not for this chicken. Let's go back to 'tother, and plan her out."

And so we did. We drove back to a point from which we could get a bird's-eye view of the whole place, and while we ate our sandwiches my companions talked. How they talked! Their conversation would have been an object lesson for the students of an agricultural college, for most of our politicians, and for all those who consider that the British farmer is not a business man. The gist of it was to grass down the existing arable land to temporary ley; to plough up a lot of the existing poor grass land, take a corn crop from it, and then later to grass it with a suitable mixture; to begin with two outdoor milking herds; and, most important of all, to get rid of the rabbits. Apparently, in their opinion, rabbits are Farming's Enemy Number One, and if they take this farm the rabbits on it will be in for a bad time.

But one thing stood out in all their talk—they wished to improve the farm and to increase its production. That should always be the driving force behind farming, and farming policy in this country should always be directed to enabling our farmers to get a living by doing just that.

* * * * * *

For some time now I have been conscious that my milking outfit has been getting rather shabby, and that it is definitely old-fashioned. It was one of the first ones made and sold by that mechanical genius at Wexcombe, Mr. A. J. Hosier, and it has milked my cows satisfactorily twice daily ever since I purchased it in 1928. There is still several years of good work in it, but, as I get so many visitors to this farm, I decided some months ago to buy the latest model as soon as I could find a customer for the old one.

Last week I managed to dispose of it, and yesterday the new one was delivered and the old one was taken away this morning. Naturally we were all very proud of the new outfit this afternoon when we used it for the first time, but the cows were not at all pleased. They missed their old friend, and we had the dickens of a job to get them to walk into the new milking shed. However, after much patient coaxing—shouting and force is worse than useless in dealing with any animals—we managed this satisfactorily; and now that they have found that the strange shed contains cake there should be no further difficulty.

There is no doubt at all that this method of milking, if properly handled, does make it comparatively easy to produce clean milk. The milk is drawn from the udder and deposited in the churn under vacuum, never coming into contact with the air at all, and thus getting little chance of outside contamination; while the steam boiler makes the sterilisation of all the machinery and utensils an easy business. There are few industries which have made greater improvements in their methods during the past ten years than has the dairying side of British farming.

* * * * * *

It is curious how most people's ideas concerning right and wrong vary according to the circumstances. Most of us frown upon dishonesty and sharp practice and law-breaking as a general rule, but most of us make exceptions. For instance, successfully to bilk the income tax authorities is generally accepted as the thing to do if possible; to buy or sell tickets in the Irish Sweepstake, both illegal, is a thing to boast about; while tales of the cute horse-dealer always go down well in any company. The other day a friend told me a glorious tale concerning a horse-dealer, a Bishop, and a Bishop's wife. I can hardly believe it to be true, but it is worth setting down.

The Bishop possessed an oldish pony, which had transported him and his wife about the diocese for several years. With the coming of the motor-car the pony was superseded and the Bishop and his good lady decided to sell it. The price to be obtained did not matter half so much as that the pony must be assured of a good home. Very quickly this got to the ears of the local horse-dealer, who straightway called on the Bishop. He purchased the pony for five pounds, and assured his lordship that the animal should have a good home. Next day he took the pony forty miles away and sold it for fifteen pounds.

A few weeks later he met the Bishop's wife, who inquired about the pony's welfare. "Well, mum," said the dealer, "that were a bad deal fer me. A week atter I got thic pony 'ome I found un dead in stable one marnin'. I 'low as 'ee must a pined away like droo missin' you an' his lordship. I didn't like to let 'ee know, as I knew you were so fond ov 'im. But 'tis a loss to a poor man like I."

"Oh, I'm so sorry!" answered the lady. "Poor Peter! I expect you are right, and that he missed us. But I don't want you to be the loser. If you will promise me that you won't tell the Bishop, I'll make up your loss."

The dealer promised that he would be as secret as the grave, pocketed the good lady's five pounds, and thanked her profusely for her generosity. Ten days later he met the Bishop, who also inquired about the pony, and to whom he told the same story. Whereupon the Bishop, after extracting a promise that the business should be kept secret from his wife, parted with yet another fiver.

It is a good story, but definitely it does not match with my experience of horse-dealers, for I have always found them as honest as most of us. I suppose if one went about one's dealing with them as if one knew all there was to know about horses, that they would be quite willing to play that game, and that they would win. But I have always assumed them to be anxious to deal honestly with me, and as yet I have not been let down.

In the country it is difficult to make dishonesty pay; at least, for very long. The trouble is that you have to live and die in close proximity to your neighbours, and therefore one crooked deal will crab future business for many years over a wide district. The motto of rural business can be best illustrated by the remark made to my father many years ago by a local builder in reply to his demand for an estimate of some proposed job. "Lor bless 'ee, Mr. Street. You lave that to we. We shain't 'urt 'ee." Country folk stay put, and therefore are forced to do business with each other continuously throughout their lives, and also to meet each other socially out of business hours. Consequently it does not pay to hurt one another. A low form of business morality possibly, but it works, and on this score has much to recommend it.

February

To-day, the first of February, calamity descended upon the youngest member of my household, my small daughter of thirteen. For some time she had been complaining of headaches after doing her homework, so this afternoon she visited the oculist, who said firmly that all homework must cease for a year, and that she would have to wear spectacles.

Homework was no great loss apparently, but to realise that she would be compelled to wear glasses knocked all the stuffing out of her. Such a disfigurement, I suppose, is a much bigger grief to a girl than to a boy, but her woebegone appearance reminded me of how I suffered at about the same age when I happened to be forced to wear at school something odd in the way of clothes. I remembered that awful feeling of being different from my companions, and the ever-present sense of inferiority which went with it. A physical difference must be even more trying to a child, I decided, so I racked my brains to try to find some way of making life appear a trifle brighter to my daughter, and suggested to her that now homework was taboo, possibly a pony to ride in the evenings might fill the gap.

Her response to this suggestion was such that I have been kicking myself for my selfishness up to date. Apparently, to ride has been her life's ambition, and her small heart could scarce contain her joy at the thought that this was to be realised in the near future. She went off to bed thinking that she possessed the best father in the world, when, in truth, I am one of the most selfish. Why have I not suggested riding to her before? Expense is no reason, for the cost of keeping a child's pony on a farm is negligible, and the facilities for learning to ride are obvious. No! The reason is because I am not only selfish, but also a coward.

I have a notion that the majority of parents are like unto me with respect to their offspring. We infer to our children that we are forbidding them to do this, that, or the other for their own good, when in reality it is to save ourselves worry. Our greater experience makes us aware of the possible dangers, and our greater age magnifies these to a very appreciable extent. Consequently, we try to prevent our children from taking any risk whatsoever, not because of the risk itself, but because of the anxiety its taking will cause us.

But what is the good? We get older and so do our children, and they must live their own lives. I know that for my daughter to learn to ride will entail a certain amount of danger, but so will driving a car, meeting young men, and all sorts of other things which she will be bound to do as she grows up. I once heard a friend remark that his wife was keeping their small infant "hermetically sealed," and often I have laughed with scorn at many parents who would not let their children do this or that. Now I find that I am—or, rather, have been—in the same category. I will remain in it no longer. My own child is growing up, whether I like it or not, and, within reason, she must be permitted to live her own life.

All that sounds very casual. The only child wants a pony—well, let her have one. But in reality it is far from casual, for I can see that the future will be full of worry. I wonder if it is because Pam is an only child that I feel like this? Does the father of six and over worry less? Possibly he becomes a trifle philosophical over the sixth, but I imagine that he goes through the same tribulations with his first-born. Another thing which puzzles me is why her mother is all for this pony business. She used to hunt years ago, and therefore she knows the dangers as well as I do. Is it that she has more courage or more common sense than I? Possibly both, but, anyway, I am definitely committed. If a pony to ride will satisfy Pam's ambition up to date, and also help her to forget the handicap of spectacles, she shall have one, and to-morrow I must see about finding a suitable animal.

To-day was a Saturday, and therefore Pam was home from school. She made tentative inquiries at breakfast as to just how one bought a pony, and I told her that the best plan was to inquire of one's friends, and that the previous evening I had mentioned to a friend over the telephone that I was looking out for the Archangel Gabriel in pony shape at a reasonable price. " This sort of business takes time, Pam," I told her. " You can't buy a pony in a shop, so you'll just have to wait in patience."

But I was mistaken. Rural communication is a swiftish business. We had a whole crowd of people to tea this afternoon, when the maid came in to say that my friend and another gentleman were in the study; and there I found him in company with another very good friend of mine, a horse-dealer of considerable local repute. The dealer told me that he had just the very pony for Pam, but when I inquired the price he looked sheepish.

" You know, tidn' no good dealin' when you be with Mr. So-and-So," he said. " You see, 'ee wur with me when I bought the pony. I gi'ed so much fer un, an' you kin 'ave 'im fer a pound more. 'Tis givin' 'im away reely, but wot kin I do? "

What indeed, I thought, for I knew both these jokers intimately. " Well, the price is all right," I said to the dealer, " but you'd better come into the other room and talk to the ladies. I'm a back number in this business. You'll have to explain to Pam's mother that this pony is safe and quiet. Come and have some tea."

The dealer was in loud check riding breeches and had a

muffler round his neck, and this attire seemed to worry him a trifle. "I bain't got up fer comp'ny," he protested. "An' you got a lot of folks in t'other room, 'cause I zeed 'em droo the winder." "Folks be sugared," I said. "Tea's ready, and you'll have to settle this business with my wife." "Well, all right then," he said. "I kin do wi' a cup o' tea, an' I've a got round a main vew wimmen in me time."

When we entered the drawing-room he gave me an object lesson in manners. There were at least a dozen people there, mostly ladies, and all strangers to him, but he was not a whit abashed. He came in, shook hands with my wife, and then beamed a cheery good-day to the whole company. Then he sat down in their midst and entertained them all, while my friend and I took a back seat. I forget the whole list of the pony's virtues and the many tales of horses and horse-dealing which he told us, but he made tea a riotous meal for everybody. The expression on Pam's face as she waited on him and drank in his every word was too wonderful.

"This yer pony, missie, be jist the very thing fer you," he told her. "His name's Toby, an' 'ee's a little gentleman." My wife and all the ladies present backed him up, and my pupil, resplendent in breeches and tops, sided with the majority. I was as wax in their hands, and after tea a car-load of us drove to the dealer's home, where I bought the pony and my daughter had her first ride. My pupil is going to fetch Toby home to-morrow morning, and my small daughter will not sleep a wink to-night.

* * * * * *

This morning, as we were waiting for Toby's arrival, I could not help wondering whether buying him was wise. That it will be a good thing for his little mistress, I know, but her dealer friend told her yesterday that in a week or two he would have me riding again. Also he told me so. "You be gettin' fat," he said.

"Too fat an' too soft. Do 'ee a power o' good to ride a bit every day. When the little missie kin ride I shall bring a 'oss over fer you." I am desperately afraid that he will make me ride, for he has what folks call "a way with him." And I have not been across a horse since Pam was born! Ugh! What purgatory may lie in store!

Toby arrived in good shape just before lunch. He is a nicely made pony with a good forehand, a thing which I like to see in a saddle-horse; otherwise it is downhill all the way. After lunch a neighbour's little boy turned up on his pony. There is a freemasonry about horses, and, having heard that Pam had a pony, he had come down to help in the good work. The riding school was held in a soft pasture. I was relegated to the lowly post of groom, whilst my infant, very proud in an old pair of breeches once worn by her mother, drank in words of wisdom from her youthful teachers.

She has had her first lesson; she has fallen off once; but her appetite at tea was unimpaired. Her father is now realising what his parents suffered some thirty years ago owing to his youthful escapades. He is also wishing that children did not grow up. Very little girls are undiluted pleasure, but a lanky child of thirteen careering about on a pony is a definite responsibility.

* * * * * *

I have not written in this diary for several days because life has been far too busy a business. To the cares of a farm, a milking herd of nearly a hundred cows, the trials and troubles connected with writing and broadcasting, add those which come from an enthusiastic daughter with her first pony, and every day is a day like a week. To-day is Sunday, which does grant time to stick down a few notes on the past week.

All the pony business last week-end had put me behind with my work, so Monday was a day of hurried farming and harassed writing. Tuesday was the same, with the addition of a bad calving case just to make life interesting. Still, late that night I was able to write "finis" to the coming broadcast talk on W. H. Hudson, and went to bed feeling that I had earned my corn—how horsy I am becoming since Toby arrived—and that I could face my agent in London without shame on the morrow.

Wednesday I spent in town on necessary business, stayed the night, and returned home at 5.30 on Thursday. Thursday was Pam's half-day, and I knew she was going riding. In the train I imagined all sorts of things, but I found her all in one piece on Salisbury platform, thank heaven! She told me that she had fallen off again, but that her teacher had told her that she was getting on. It sounded a trifle Irish, but there was no mistaking her joy. Henceforth I am to take a back seat in her affections, I fear. Toby comes first and my pupil, her riding master, second.

Friday was a day of catching up with correspondence and farming matters, together with a long conversation with our County Agricultural Organiser, during which I bragged about the efficiency of my new milking outfit. Alas! this was a case of pride going before a fall. On Saturday morning at 5.30 a.m. I was awakened by the sound of some gravel which Charlie had thrown against my window, and I looked out to be told that the pulsator on the milking machine would not function.

As I dressed I remembered that it was at least a year since Charlie had been compelled to bother me with any mechanical difficulty, which speaks well for him and also for his outfit. In this case, having only a week or two's experience of the new machine, he had, quite rightly, refused to tinker with it himself, and had come straight down for me. But when I turned out it was bitter cold, and the stiffest frost we have had this year. Why, oh why, is it that this sort of thing always happens in bad weather?

As we were driving up to the downs I thought that I knew precious little about the new machinery, but I comforted myself with the remembrance of what I had once heard one of my men say to a new hand: "You do want to watch out fer the guvnor. 'Ee don't like work, but 'ee kin do it ef 'ee's force put." Yesterday morning I was undoubtedly "force put," but also I was lucky. In a few moments I spotted that a set screw had worked loose. I tightened it up with a spanner, started the engine, and all was well. Luck, I grant, but how impressive! Just call the guvnor and he puts things right in a moment. I shall be able to live on Saturday's triumph for several months. That same evening Charlie and I met again, this time at the Annual Dinner of the Agricultural Workers' Union. And yet some folks think the country dull! Why, it is one continuous round of exciting happenings.

So much for the past week. This morning, Sunday, my pupil, having managed to borrow a fiery steed, went off riding on his own, so I was promoted to the position of riding-master. To do the lad justice, he wanted to take Pam riding by his side on a leading rein, but her mother took one look at his horse and decreed otherwise. So Pam and I and Toby went to a small pasture, where I sat on a fallen tree and let her ride round and round the field, off the leading rein and on her own for the first time.

No one will ever know what I suffered during the process. Undoubtedly Pam is getting on famously, for she seemed quite capable of managing her pony at the trot; but when he broke into a canter my heart was in my mouth. However, we have crossed that bridge satisfactorily. Granted there was considerable daylight between her small behind and the saddle, but she returned to me breathless, saying: " Oh, Daddy, he cantered, and I didn't fall off. It was lovely!" And from that moment until lunch Toby was forced to learn that life had become a much more arduous business.

Now that Pam can ride safely on her own the idea of a safe, very safe and quiet, cob on which to accompany her seems to be rather attractive. My dealer friend has promised me an absolute armchair. How I shall suffer even if he is as good as his word—but what odds? I shall be suffering in a good cause for two reasons. My daughter says that it will be just splendid, and my wife remarks that it will get my weight down; but, even so, I could wish that the process was not going to be so painful. It occurs to me that all this riding business can be traced to my taking a pupil who is mad keen on horses. Have I been harbouring a traitor? Have I been led up the garden by that innocent-looking, shy boy? Whether or no, that lad shall do some work next week. Yea, verily!

* * * * * *

I like the way Spring comes to this Wiltshire country, or, rather, I like the occasional day of Spring which always comes to cheer us in February. To-morrow is always so much more important than yesterday that at every season of the year I go to bed wondering about it: but in February I look forward to each to-morrow with special eagerness, for in February any to-morrow may be that glorious foretaste of Spring which this month never fails to grant. Even if March arrives to greet a frozen world there will have been one whiff of Spring in February. Experience has taught me to look for this on any day after the fourteenth of February, and to-day it arrived—the first day of Spring. As usual it came suddenly, without warning, like a thief in the night. Yesterday was Winter, cold and dour, but to-day has been Spring, laughing and gay.

The magic of it crept through the open window into my study, telling me that Spring was waiting outside. I leaned out of the window intending merely to take one peep at her before I settled down to work, but it was the old story—the woman tempted me. The lawn and pasture beyond glistened a bright green in the sunlight after the night's rain ; there was little wind ; a thrush sang gaily in the lime tree ; a starling chuckled throatily on the stable roof, while white clouds billowed across a bright blue sky. Out of doors seemed to offer much too friendly a welcome to be ignored in favour of indoor work at a desk, so I wandered out into a morning which was all warm and February.

Even my conscience was in a quandary this morning. He wanted to upbraid me for laziness and shirking, and he wanted to urge me on not to miss the glory of the day. Finally, he decided in favour of laziness, and proceeded to argue in support of this decision. " Laughter is precious," he said, " and laughter is a scarce article. Not yet has man increased the world's output of this valuable commodity by means of machinery to such an extent that he moans about over-production and surplus. Laughter is a natural thing. Laughter is a gift which man should accept gratefully from whatever source it comes. This morning Spring is laughing gaily everywhere, in the meadows, on the downs, and along the lane. Remember, laughter is infectious ; you should try to catch it at every opportunity. Now is a good chance. Now, when Wiltshire's friendly countryside is laughing hand in hand with Spring, go for a walk and laugh with them for an hour or so."

A logical fellow, my conscience, and in this instance I was not fool enough to disagree with him, for his arguments and my inclinations were identical. So I set off for a walk.

I turned my back on the farm buildings and trudged up a gritty flint road leading to the downs. All around me the countryside was aware that Spring had come. From the hazel bushes in the hedgerow hung dusty yellow catkins, or lambs' tails, looking for all the world like miniature bunches of bananas. In a sheltered spot I noticed a wild honeysuckle in full leaf; in another a thrush sitting on her nest; while from the mouth of a burrow a baby rabbit regarded me with infantile solemnity as I strolled by All the hedgerow birds were busily intent upon their Spring business. They were either mating, flirting, building nests, or singing a song in praise of the day.

Everything seemed to be in twos. Pairs of pigeons flew off with tremendous clatter from the occasional roadside trees as I passed, and through the hedge I noticed a pair of partridges, who, knowing that the shooting season was over, took but little notice of me when I clambered up the bank to get a better look at them. The cock bird, easily distinguished at this time of year by the bright reddish-brown shield on his breast which is missing on the ash-grey bosom of the hen, threw up his head and stood at attention, while his wife pecked unconcernedly near him.

Presently he decided that he did not like the look of me, and away he ran over the pasture, with his drab little wife trotting meekly close behind him. Even the rook parliament of last week seemed to have dissolved itself into committees of two this morning; and these were emulating the human politicians in that they were exploring every avenue and leaving no stone or twig unturned.

I turned out of the lane on to the downs, and there I stood for awhile gazing at the valley below. Everything glistened; the grass in the meadows, the river, the water in the ditches, the slate roofs of the cottages, the plumage of a flock of peewits which were wheeling like black and white butterflies far below me, the wire fences, the electric pylons—everything in this Wiltshire valley was twinkling at the sun. There were new-born clover leaves under my feet, an amber film over the willows, a lush-green carpet in the meadows, and a green sheen on the arable fields, where the wheat was lifting its head to greet the Spring, and some hares were dancing in a most abandoned fashion.

Promise, I thought, is the message of that picture which a day like this brings to the countryside—a promise of beauty and increase which has been and always will be fulfilled for as long as the world lasts, and I congratulated my conscience on his logical arguments of an hour or so before. Whereupon he started to argue once more. " How many more times will you have this promise made to you ? " he asked. " How many more Springs can you hope to see ? Man's allotted span will grant you nearly thirty ; average luck should give you at least fifteen ; but Fate can rule that this one is to be your last."

But I refused to argue with such a depressing companion. Every year of my life I have watched the miracle of the earth reclad, a miracle which defies the art of painter or writer to describe. Why ask for more ? Why be so presumptuous as to attempt to reckon up the future like a usurer calculates his interest ? Rather let me be grateful for the glory of the Springs which I have been permitted to see, a precious possession which, while I live, cannot be taken from me by any man.

Those were my thoughts this morning, and now at 10 p.m., when it is raining hard, I hold the same view. The bounty of to-day is still fresh in my mind—to-day, when I was permitted to watch the earth donning her first garments after she had been awakened from her winter sleep by the call of a morning which was all warm and February.

* * * * * *

Most men are cowards, and most men are aware that they are

cowards. At any rate I have known all my life that I was a coward. Of course I have never told anyone about this. I have kept this knowledge strictly to myself, and presented a brave front to the world, but all the time this shameful truth has been whispered to me by my conscience. Why, then, am I ashamed no longer? Why do I dare to put it down in black and white? Simply because to-day by one act of pure heroism I have wiped out the stains of the past. There have been no glaring headlines in the papers concerning this. I have not saved anyone from death at the risk of my own life. I have not battled manfully with burglars or gangsters. I have not driven a car or an aeroplane for prodigious distances or at record speed. Nothing spectacular have I accomplished, and no modern invention has been concerned with the matter. All I have done is to ride a horse for two hours—and when I say ride, I do not mean broncho-busting, steeplechasing, or hunting even, but merely a little quiet, sedate hacking. A very ordinary thing to many people, perhaps, but in my case it was such an exhibition of courage that even my conscience is speechless with admiration.

Since my small daughter started riding there have been many hints thrown out by friends and enemies that I ought to get a hack and take her out with me, but until this morning I had safely ignored them. Indeed, I had arranged for her dealer friend to take her out to-day, but the blighter rang up at breakfast-time to say that he could not get over, whereupon his intended companion's face fell a full yard. Then, on the instant, the hero, I myself, stepped into the breach. Why, I cannot quite make out. If I had taken time to think I should never have done so, but courage and thought do not go together.

Without thinking of the enormity of the risk I offered to take her out, and immediately rang up a nearby riding-school, asking for a very quiet mount—lots of emphasis on the quiet—

which must be up to my weight. They promised to send such a paragon round, and during the intervening half-hour I repented of my rashness whilst my daughter exulted. How I suffered! Forty-two years old, sixteen stone, and my last ride fully thirteen years behind me. However, a promise to a child is a promise which has to be kept; so, when a huge beast of at least sixteen hands pawed the gravel outside, I had to face the music or be forever shamed. Clad in an old pair of slacks, I clambered into the saddle amidst loud cheers from my ribald household.

Never have I felt such a fool as I did for about thirty seconds, but when we got going into a comfortable lope up the grass track leading to the downs I began to enjoy myself: and from that moment the morning was pure bliss. Pam's open admiration of her father added greatly to the pleasure. "But, Daddy," she burst out, after we had gone about two hundred yards, "you can ride." Respect for their elders is all too lacking in modern children, so I countered with: "But, my dear child, what have I told you for many years?"

But I enjoyed that ride. Granted there was nothing classy in my riding. Most men cannot resist showing off a trifle when they are in the saddle, but I was modesty itself. Any showing off, I thought, will be done by the old horse, but not if I can prevent it. So I watched him carefully every step of the way, in case he should take it into his head to revert to childish practices. But I need not have worried. He realised from the outset that he was carrying very precious freight, and from first to last he behaved like the gentleman he looks.

But if I did not show off while riding, I must confess that I went indoors to lunch with a decided swagger. Also, whenever my conscience sees fit to chide me in the future, I shall remind him of my bravery of this morning. And how stiff I shall be to-morrow! To-night I went upstairs to wish Pam good-night and tuck her up. We talked of our riding for awhile, and as I left the room a sleepy, happy voice murmured : " Oh, Daddy, I'm having too good a time." Herein I have my reward.

* * * * * *

For my sins I get all sorts of people calling on me asking advice as to how to make farming pay handsomely, and also many who take up my time in just grousing about present conditions. It was a pleasant change this afternoon to have a conversation with a youngish farmer who was quite satisfied with life. I had already heard something of his farming career from one of his neighbours, and had gathered that this young man had succeeded during a period when so many farmers had failed by practising those two rather old-fashioned virtues, hard work and thrift. The fact that he had worked hard was evident in his general appearance, but the chief reason for his financial success was due to his thrifty way of living. He told me that he had started with very little capital, and that his first herd of cows was bought on the hire-purchase system. This sort of thing usually means disaster, for it is difficult to farm without sufficient capital to stock the holding. But this man had married an extraordinary wife, and, as far as I could make out, the two of them had spent their honeymoon and their first year together living in a small hut on top of the downs. Apparently he had been dairyman, his wife had been second man, and they had thoroughly enjoyed that first year in this fashion. Since that date they have progressed by easy stages from the hut to a fairly large farmhouse, living in better and better cottages as they made their way upwards financially.

To-day that road of progress for the young farmer with respect to his living accommodation cannot be too strongly stressed. Start in a cottage and you finish in the manor house. Start in the manor house and you will finish in the workhouse.

In the latter case the progress will be decidedly the swifter. The number of comparatively young farmers who should trace their financial failure to starting life in a large farmhouse with two acres of walled-in garden alongside is legion. The small amount of capital required to-day to stock a farm is not sufficient to warrant the young farmer living in a house which necessitates an income of at least a thousand a year to keep it up decently.

Of course there is another side to this business. Old habits are not easily broken, and too often the man who starts in a small way by living cheaply in a cottage cannot enjoy life in the manor house later on when his financial position makes this not only possible but imperative. Which is a pity, for the countryside suffers when the farmer who *can* afford to keep up these large farmhouses refuses to do so. The whole business boils down to that old saying: " Cut your coat according to the cloth."

* * * * * *

What a change has taken place in the farming of this district since my boyhood—or, rather, since my young manhood! Years ago this district was all hurdled sheep and corn; now it is all cows, pigs, poultry, and grass sheep, with only a small amount of corn. As a result the countryside is nothing like so picturesque, but the new type of farming is more suited to the times, and also works in better with our climate. I can remember the time when I should have been cursing the wet weather we have been having during the past week or two, because then I should have been worrying about the sowing of a hundred acres of Spring corn. Now I look at my pastures and meadows with satisfaction, for this season I am heavily stocked with cattle and rather short of hay. However, the grass in the meadows and the general earliness of everything this Spring looks as though I shall not have to buy any hay. Last year at this date I was compelled to buy half a rick from a neighbour. Another neighbour wanted the other half, so we first agreed upon the price for the rick, and then the seller left the two buyers to divide it as they thought fit. We did so, I remember, by that ancient method of one making the division and the other choosing his portion. I do not think there is any better way.

As I was driving along a country lane this afternoon—I was going to buy a bull—I saw a man thatching a large barn. The new thatch looked such a bright gold against the dull leaden sky and the blue-black tarred road, that I should imagine the wheat crop from which it was made had been harvested without one spot of rain. Such straw makes the best thatch. It is easier to draw and it lasts much longer as thatch than that made from straw which has taken a lot of rain.

A nice job, thatching, a satisfying job, for the craftsman who does it must be aware that he is doing something which very few of his fellows can accomplish. Even to-day, when thatch is fast disappearing from our villages, the local thatcher is a bit of an autocrat. He works as and when he thinks fit, and society in rural districts, from the highest to the lowest, must await his pleasure and convenience. Even great wealth does not enable anyone to order the house-thatcher to come ; its possessor must needs ask humbly. In other words, while the competent house-thatcher may not amass great wealth, he achieves status, a much finer thing than wealth, although modern civilisation does not seem to regard it so.

I bought my bull, a nice little roan chap about fifteen months old, and he is to be delivered by lorry to-morrow. Driving home, I tried to recall all the bull escapades with which I had been connected, and discovered that since I have let the bull run loose with my cows escapades with bulls have been almost non-existent. Before this, we were always having them. I have been dragged for yards along the road while helping to lead home a

refractory bull from market. Once I had to get up a loft and lasso an irate bull who had got loose in his box below, and who defied anyone to come in and argue with him. And I can remember a man being killed by a bull and my father shooting the animal when I was a very small boy. There is no doubt that the old-time solitary confinement of bulls had much to answer for with regard to their bad temper, for now they run loose we do not take any special notice of them at all.

And still it rains, but March comes in to-morrow, which should give us some dust and its accompanying east wind. Well, a fortnight's dry weather and we—or, rather, the cows—will be out at grass. Which reminds me that I must remember to tell Jim to shut the water out of the meadows, which must be dry under foot for grazing. Otherwise the cows will have five mouths when they are turned out—one consuming mouth and four trampling feet.

March

From what I can gather from her conversation, the most important need of the present day, in Pam's opinion, is a suitable hack for her father. I have agreed to this in so far as to saying that I will buy one when a beast can be found which shall satisfy three essential requirements. It must be cheap to buy—this is very important; it must be up to my weight—this is more important; and it must be dog quiet—this, of course, is most important. As a concession to feminine importunity, I have made two or three inquiries for such a paragon from some of my horsey friends, all of whom, to my annoyance, shouted with laughter at the very thought of me on a horse of any kind. Their amusement was such that I began to doubt whether I had been wise in letting them know my intentions, for most of their ideas of humour are based on the fundamental principle of the discomfiture of the other fellow. So the other day I bought a copy of *Horse and Hound* in order to see whether its advertisement columns contained news of a suitable mount.

From the time that paper came into my house I did not have a moment's peace. Pam and my pupil had their heads bent over it at every opportunity, and read aloud all the advertisements of quiet horses suitable for nervous riders of either sex. In order to silence these gibes I replied to one advertisement which offered two quiet hacks at a low price to a good home. In due course I received a letter stating that their owner, a lady, having read some of my books, was prepared to let me have both horses for their keep if I would agree to return them to her should the time come when I no longer required them. After this I must admit that being an author has its advantages.

However, this offer, of course, left me no way out, so to-day I drove up to Sussex to inspect the horses.

I found them to be two old hunters, both up to my weight, quiet both in stable and out, and, as far as I could see, sound on their pins and in their wind. It was obvious that they were pets and that it was a wrench for their owner to have to part with them. But she was giving up riding and going abroad, and all she wanted was to be sure that her old friends should have a good home and not, as she put it, be allowed to come down in the world. So I gladly agreed to take them and to look after them well, and to allow their owner to call and see them whenever she wished to do so. I am sending a horse-box for them in two days' time, but what their owner will do when her horses depart, I cannot think.

* * * * * *

For better or worse the two nags, Peter and Glory, arrived this evening about six o'clock, together with a copious amount of rugs and saddlery, and a pathetic note saying that this was a gift, and informing me also of the horses' likes and dislikes. It ended up with : " And Peter is very fond of apples ! "

What could I do ? To offer to pay for the saddlery now would be insulting, and not to try and make some little response to such courteous generosity would be rudeness of the worst type. So I did three things. Firstly, I saw to it that Pam fetched three apples and gave one to Peter, one to Glory, and one to her beloved Toby ; secondly, I wrote a letter of thanks to their owner, telling her that her old friends had arrived safely, and drove into Salisbury to post it in order that she would be sure to receive it next morning ; and thirdly, I packed up a parcel of my books to send to her next day.

But books are a poor return for horses. Granted, I wanted to get hold of a hack as cheaply as possible, but there is a limit to even my stinginess. "Peter is very fond of apples!" Blast it! I feel like a thief.

* * * * * *

Unbeknown to Pam I ordered a pair of Jodhpurs some days ago, and this morning they arrived, so I came down to breakfast arrayed ready to ride. She surveyed me for a few moments, as I thought in admiration, for careful examination in the looking-glass upstairs had failed to reveal any serious flaws in my appearance. But she surveyed me in silence for so long that I was constrained to ask her ladyship's opinion.

"We-e-ll, they're all right, Daddy, I suppose, but somehow I don't quite like you in them. I know what it is, your bottom part's too young."

After all I have done for that young woman, too! God knows, I did not think my top part looked exactly ancient, but now I know, for out of the mouths of young children comes truth. Still, I was one up on her this morning. She had to catch a bus for school immediately after breakfast, but I was going to ride Peter for the first time. Green with envy, she ran off down the road, while my pupil and I went over to the stable to saddle up.

We had a good ride this morning together, and in the afternoon went out again in company with Pam, home for her half-day, and her dealer friend. Both horses are toppers. They may be old—according to my daughter, so am I—but they do not look old; they go like youngsters and behave beautifully. The dealer's face when he learned how much they had cost me was a study. For a man in his district to get hold of such horses for nothing was entirely against his creed.

I cannot write any more to-night. I may think that I do not look old, but my present stiffness after to-day's riding proves to me that I am old, very old. It will be an effort for me to get upstairs to bed. But it was fun riding to-day, and somehow the sight of those three wise heads, Peter's, Glory's, and Toby's, poking out over the half-doors of their respective boxes makes me feel that a little of the old glory has returned to Ditchampton Farm, despite its accompaniment of aches and pains. (Note.—All three like apples, so I shall have to plant an orchard.)

* * * * * *

To-day is Sunday, and both to-day and yesterday brought weather not fit for a dog to be out in. I had an article published a year ago under the title of "March is a Man," and, by gum! the way in which he has blustered the last day or two told everybody that he was a man and a very rude man at that. How I do not like his east wind! More so this year than ever, because now I have three horses in stable, which have to be exercised daily.

It takes a peculiar brand of cold courage to take the rug off a sixteen-hand hunter first thing after breakfast in this sort of weather. At least, it requires the sort of courage of which I have but little. Although I faced the ordeal yesterday morning, to-day I funked it. What would have been fun to Peter might have been death to me, and I prefer to die warm if possible, certainly not when my bones feel brittle and the only part of me which sweats is my nose. However, this horrible east wind has done some good. It has dried up the sodden fallows which February left behind, and enabled farming to begin its Spring manœuvres in which to-day most of the units taking part have been mechanised.

Funny how one's daily doings affect one's writing. This morning my wife and I drove over to lunch with some friends near Tidworth, who took us first to see the Church Parade, and then a tour of the camp. Hence the military phrase concerning farming operations. Somehow there is something about the pomp and panoply of the army which thrills one, although in these days it is difficult to find anybody who wishes for war.

God knows, I don't, and yet I cannot agree with the people who yearn for total disarmament on our part, no matter what happens in other countries. I cannot help thinking of my school days. Rules and regulations and agreements played their useful parts in that little world doubtless, but, unless the sixth could have used force when necessary, and every boy knew that the sixth would use force if necessary, the school could not have been carried on. Also I remember that a strong sixth form made for a complete absence of bullying, and that a weak sixth had exactly the opposite effect.

But, even so, I cannot swallow this dictator business, and I am wondering just how long the people on the Continent will stand for it. From all accounts their trouble is that they don't know how to laugh, which reminds me of a good story which I heard this morning. A doctor went to heaven, where he was greeted by St. Peter, who asked him what had been his occupation on earth. When he replied that he had been a doctor in an asylum, St. Peter said: " Come along with me. You are just the man we want." " Why? What's the trouble?" asked the doctor. " Serious trouble," answered St. Peter. " The Almighty thinks he's Hitler!" A trifle irreverent for a Sunday entry, perhaps, but how I wish someone would tell it to Herr Hitler! But I suppose the teller would not live long afterwards.

But to return to Tidworth. The village and camp are called Tidworth, but the local pack of hounds is known as the Tedworth, and this morning I discovered the reason. Apparently, the village used to be Tedworth also, but when the powers that be decided to build a camp there, the first plan and survey contained a mistake in the spelling of the name, and that mistake has now become permanent.

* * * * * *

Cold though it is the countryside is high busy. March is always a busy month for farmers, for February is usually too wet or too frosty for cultivation, and, in most districts, April is on the late side for sowing Spring corn. Consequently, in March there always seem to be more jobs to be done on a farm than can possibly be done in time.

Still, I suppose we modern farmers have an easier time at this season than did our ancestors; for we have mechanical power at our disposal, while they were forced to rely solely on the horse. To-day there is no doubt at all that most farms in this country are being run mainly by machinery, and that the horse is fast disappearing from our fields. Many people say that this is a pity, and I have heard some folk say firmly that it should not be allowed. It is easy to sympathise with their desire to bring back the horse and, therefore, the old-time romance and beauty to the rural scene, but I do not think that the British farmer is treated fairly by public opinion concerning this.

If he does try his hardest to make his farm pay by using every device placed at his disposal by modern invention, with the inevitable result of a corresponding diminution in the man-power on his farm, he is told on all sides that he is a dirty dog. If he does not do this, but carries on in the old way, using no modern machinery, the same critics point the finger of scorn at him, and say: "How can you expect farming to pay when it is run on such old-fashioned lines?"

But most farmers do not worry very much about these ill-informed criticisms. They know that whatever they do they will not succeed in pleasing everybody, so, very wisely, they are trying to please themselves by using modern machinery on their farms as and when they think it advisable. By doing this they may lose the sympathy of the public, but if by using machinery in place of horses they can make their farming pay they will gain its respect. To my mind the respect of the public is of much greater value than its sympathy.

Possibly the whole of this island's farming has not yet been mechanised, for much of the land is too hilly for mechanical transport, but in the south of England the March landscape is now filled with machinery of all kinds. Tractors and old motor-cars are now busily hauling all sorts of implements, and plodding horses are few and far between. Drills, harrows, cultivators, ploughs, manure distributors, rollers, and many other farming tools are being hauled up and down the mellowed fields of England by mechanical power.

Sometimes I wonder whether this mechanisation has made the work of the farm labourer any easier or not. Granted, it has greatly reduced the actual hard, tiring manual labour, but even with its aid a lot of farm work is still both hard and tiring. For instance, the lot of the carter walking behind a team of horses during the past week or two has been infinitely to be preferred to that of the tractor driver sitting on his vibrating steed for long hours in the biting east wind. Think of it! Eight hours daily, sitting hunched up on the iron seat of a tractor which is moving at about three, at the most four, miles per hour over the open country, exposed to the wind and with the dust whipping into one's eyes. A man who does that will be dog-tired at the end of the day, and will most certainly earn his wages.

So here I would like to pay a well-earned tribute to the British agricultural labourer for the admirable way in which he has taken to all the mechanical inventions that economic conditions have forced into his daily life during the past few years. It is true that any engineer can drive a tractor, and that a carter can plough; but to plough by mechanical means requires that the knowledge of both engineering and ploughing shall be possessed by one man. The only man who can accomplish this difficult task is an agricultural labourer; for, while it is comparatively easy to teach him to be a competent engineer, it is well-nigh impossible to teach the average competent engineer the art and mystery of ploughing. And it is the quality of the ploughing which matters to farming. The tractor is merely the motive power.

Therefore, I would ask any townsman who travels through the countryside this March to notice the work of the modern farm labourer. Whenever you see a man hunched up on a tractor, a man dressed in very shabby clothes with perhaps some empty bags used as an extra overcoat, making him look almost like a Robinson Crusoe, take your hat off to him. Watch his progress up that long straight furrow. Notice that he has one eye forward, one eye backwards to his plough, and another eye looking all around him. In spite of this extra eye he is no monster, but merely the best type of farm workman in this year of grace 1935, a skilled engineer and a skilled farm labourer; or, as I would describe him, the salt of the earth.

In another field, perhaps, you will find him cultivating ploughed land, harrowing it, rolling it, or sowing seed. In a grass field he will be chain-harrowing, rolling, or distributing manure. But, almost invariably, he will be doing this by means of mechanical power, for, as I say, the horse is vanishing from our fields. The progress of civilisation has meant that this change has had to take place, and it is useless for anyone either to try to stop it or to mourn it too deeply. We should comfort ourselves with the thought that the land remains unaltered—the same canvas upon which our forefathers painted a lovely picture by their farming operations. To-day we paint the same picture, but we use modern brushes.

In April we shall see the result of our March painting. Then those barren fields over which the modern farm labourer is now driving modern implements will change their appearance. One fine morning there will be a faint green sheen over them, a sheen which was not there the day before. As April advances with her sun and showers this green sheen will grow into a lush-green carpet, so soothing to the eye that we shall forget the barren landscape over which March blustered with his nasty but necessary east wind.

* * * * * *

How long will it take for my old bones and muscles to become acclimatised to riding? For ten days I have suffered purgatory, and even now one of my kidneys seems to be adhering to my spine and getting a sharp tug with every motion of my mount. "The best thing for the inside of a man is the outside of a horse." I do not know who wrote those words, but, while I am ready to admit their truth, how I would like to meet him! To all my friends and relations my sufferings are a huge joke, and even Pam cannot understand my eagerness to ride at a walking pace at every opportunity. "I don't see why your back hurts, Daddy," she says. "My back never hurts." Neither did mine at her age, but now—ugh!

However, to-day a local point-to-point meeting brought relief from torture, and my car was filled to overflowing with eager spectators from my household, who somehow or other managed to find room for a neighbour's little boy, one of Pam's enthusiastic riding friends.

Children beat me. For some weeks now Pam has been asking permission to jump, without success. I tell her mother that we are only putting off the evil day, and that soon she will jump whether we like it or not. The devil of it is that Toby can jump, and jump well. However, I did think that if she saw a fall to-day it would curb her enthusiasm for jumping a trifle, but not a bit of it.

There must have been something more tricky about the last fence than I could see, for in every race somebody fell at it.

The Ladies Race

Of course, three and a half miles takes it out of a horse, and possibly rushing tired horses at it was the chief cause of the spills. But, anyway, every race someone came a purler. In the ladies' race one girl's horse went head over heels like a shot rabbit, but its rider picked herself up unhurt and strolled into the paddock apparently unconcerned. Pam's comment was : " You see, Daddy, she didn't hurt herself. So I can jump on Toby, can't I ? " As I say, children beat me.

Still, we all had a very jolly day, and, although my betting has been restricted to this sort of racing for many years, and although five shillings was the limit of my stake, I managed to pay all expenses as a result.

* * * * * *

As a rule it is difficult to find a good word to say for March. Generally he is such a blustering fellow that most of us are eager to see the back of him and to greet Spring and April hand in hand. But this year March is good enough for me, for this year Spring has stolen a march on April.

Early or late, each year of my life I have welcomed Spring gladly, but to-day she has all my heart. Never before in my memory has her coming been such a charming and delightful surprise. It is true that she flirted with me in characteristic fashion for just one day in February ; but the next day it rained, a few days later came frost, and soon afterwards March blustered in with his east wind, a wind so horrible that Spring fled from the countryside in terror. For three barren, uncomfortable weeks that east wind ruled over both countryside and town, indoors and outdoors and in bed almost ; for neither overcoats, fires, nor central heating seemed to be proof against it.

Then came the contrast. A few days ago Spring returned, suddenly and unexpectedly, but in such delightful fashion that I have dared to think she has come to stay. She gave the east wind his marching orders. and gentled rough March into such a likeable fellow that I have forgiven him his past rudeness. She beamed on countryside and town; she twinkled down the lane and along the busy street; she peeped into all sorts of places—lambing-pens, cowsheds, offices, and factories; and the magic of her smile must have crept into the darkest of slums.

But it was in the countryside that her arrival was most noticeable. Not a mile, not a step could you go last week without seeing plain evidence of her presence. Suddenly, in village and field it was shirt-sleeve weather. Forgotten was the biting east wind, discarded were the overcoats, the mufflers, and the sacks and bags which the tractor drivers were using as extra garments only a few days before. Brown forearms below white rolled shirt-sleeves were the order of the day. There was activity everywhere. The village blacksmith and the wheelwright were busy with urgent repairs; on ploughland and pasture tractors fussed and horses plodded as they hauled the latest types of farm implements; and gardens and allotments were as busy as beehives.

The whole countryside was in a bustle. Spring was driving everything under her dominion at full speed, and man was forced to hurry to try to keep pace with her. The farmer who reckoned at the beginning of last week that his work was well in hand, now realises that he reckoned without taking Spring into account. For suddenly one morning the blackthorn was out, and:

> "When the blackthorn blossoms white
> Sow the barley day and night."

Even so, no farmer could have grumbled at last week's weather. Instead, every farmer drove his men and horses and machines full speed ahead; while the Spring sunshine tempted the old men who were past active work to toddle out into the fields just to make sure that the young men realised the urgency of the land's needs now that Spring had come to the country.

After the past few days let no one malign the English climate. Granted, it is very changeable, but no other climate gives such glorious changes. Think of it ! A bare week ago the countryside was barren and dead ; now it is pulsating with eager life in every detail. Everything is different from last week. The feel of the earth beneath one's feet has altered. The birds are flirting and mating and singing in every tree and hedgerow. Hares are lolloping in couples all over the place. The wheat plant has its head uplifted to greet the sun, and a faint green tinge is spreading over the early-sown oat and barley fields. From every hillside comes the " maa " of young lambs and the plaintive cry of the nesting plovers as they swoop and twirl in dizzy fashion ; while on every hand the trees have wakened from their long winter sleep and are beginning to dress for the summer show.

But these are just a few details of Spring's doings during the past week. The main thing is that she is now here, and you can and must meet her in the countryside with every step you take. For country folk her coming is a call to urgent work ; but to townsfolk it must be a call to play. Surely when the sun warms the pavements it is high time for winter-worn townsfolk to get away from them for a few hours ; to visit woods and hedgerows and green grass and wild flowers ; and to watch Spring and their country cousins at work together in England's green and pleasant land. There is no more charming sight in all the world, and now, now and for the next few weeks is the time to watch it. Those townsfolk who come to see and admire, and not to spoil and rob, will be very welcome and well repaid for their journey ; for never was Spring in happier or busier mood.

Actual physical contact with the countryside is the only

thing which can bring the full consciousness of the glory of England's Spring. It is impossible to do this by means of words. They are hopeless, inadequate. How can one describe the annual miracle of the earth reclad? Little details one can get down on paper, but the flavour of England's Spring defies description. All last week one could see the Spring, hear the Spring, feel the Spring, and smell the Spring—England's Spring, the loveliest Spring in all the world.

Some of her last week's magic remains with me as I write at my desk—the warm, thick mist which veiled the morning sun; the friendly countryside all around me when the mist dispersed; the warm sleepiness of a village street; the sight of some lambs at play and the smell of the Spring sheepfold; the purple first leaves and curious scent of an elder bush; the silver-grey of a church tower and the warm yellow of a newly thatched barn in the bright sunlight; the warm hum of some gnats around my head; the gin-clear water of a Winter bourne as it flowed by the roadside; the feel of warm sun on the back of my neck; the continuous chorus of the birds; the smell of warm earth and sweaty horses; a general feeling that everything was waking up, and that the countryside was becoming greener every minute.

Little things and trivial, I admit, but together they tell me quite definitely that Spring has stolen a welcome march on April. How good it was to be in England last week and watch her do this so charmingly!

* * * * * *

I spent yesterday in Gloucestershire. The purpose of my visit was to call on some very good friends there who had promised to show me what is, I think, the only remaining team of working bullocks in the country. I here tender them my grateful thanks, not only for fulfilling that promise, but also for tearing up half the county on my behalf. Having got a poor, inoffensive Wiltshire moonraker into their hands, they saw to it that he had a very full day as well as a most enjoyable one.

But how interesting life in England is! I do not mean town life—that is just one mechanical thing after another—but country life. Go where you will into England's countryside and history will be almost sure to spill itself into your lap without any seeking on your part or warning from anyone.

An example of this occurred while I was being shown round the Royal Agricultural College near Cirencester. As its title implies, this college received its authority by Royal Charter, but I was told that unfortunately the actual Charter had been lost for many years. Then, just as I was expressing my sympathy to the Principal, one of his staff turned up with the ancient document. He told us that he had discovered it in the strong-room of the local bank, where it had been deposited many years before by the then secretary of the college, who had left no record of this transaction. Attached to the Charter was a huge circular wax seal about six inches in diameter, which, I suppose, was the Great Seal of England. The people to whom that old Charter was granted are now dead, but the Charter and the College remain, mute evidence that they builded wisely and well.

From the top of the College tower I was granted a view that one seldom sees—a view of but one thing only, a bit of the real England. In all that lovely panorama there was not a sign of any town or city, for even Cirencester was hidden by tall trees. The only thing to be seen was unspoilt Gloucestershire—just mellow fields, stone walls, good timber, grey stone villages, some of the best of the Cotswold country. Even a born and bred Wiltshireman such as I was forced to admit that Gloucestershire was a lovely county.

I should have been quite happy to have spent an hour on that tower, but to my hosts life was real and very earnest, so they hurried me away to a field in Lord Bathurst's park, where six oxen were pulling a heavy set of drags. If any smart advertising agent wants an illustration of the words "slowly but surely," he should take a photograph of those patient beasts. Also, if any student of rural education would like an assurance that the English agricultural labourer is no fool but a wise man, he might do a lot worse than to have a chat with the man who breaks, drives, and tends this apparently unwieldy team.

I must confess that I was surprised to find the oxen "harnessed" with collars and traces, as I had always imagined them to be "yoked." Surely the strength of the ox is in his head? At least, whenever I have to deal with a refractory bull and he gets his head down, I am well aware that such is the case. My friends told me that since the War some yoked oxen were used for ploughing in Sussex, but that for some years now that county had abandoned oxen entirely in favour of horses and tractors. Yet another form of farm power thrown by progress into the discard of history. Still, these harnessed oxen were a splendid sight, and I can imagine that they would appear even more splendid when hitched to a plough. Some day I must drive up again and try to see them ploughing—or, rather, see them performing the most spectacular and the most beautiful of all farming operations.

The economics of oxen as against horses for farm work are beyond me, but my energetic college friends seemed to think that on actual costings the oxen would win, and told me that they might even make an experiment to find out for certain. It seemed very strange to hear them arguing about this in such a setting. A broad expanse of ploughed land surrounded by woods, over which six huge horned beasts plodded and plodded and plodded, did not seem to match remarks like "Sixty per

cent. of horse speed, I grant, but against that you have the lower cost of feeding and upkeep." The sight of draught oxen at work brought back to me memories of Bible stories, in which, if I have not forgotten my mother's teaching, there was no cent. per cent.

However, oxen, economics, the Gloucestershire countryside, and the company of my friends, together made up a delightful day, and I was sorry when the time came to say good-bye to them. But before I left I managed to obtain the inside information concerning the correct pronunciation of that difficult word Cirencester. The natives call it SIRENSESTER, so I take it that it is correct, for surely they should know the rights of it. Highbrows from afar call it SISSESTER, which, I was told, is hopelessly wrong. Apparently, if you dislike the native pronunciation,

SISSETER will pass muster, but in future I shall plump for the local SIRENSESTER.

But these differences in pronunciation must make it rather fun for the local telephone exchange. I wonder if the girls employed there take full advantage of it. When anyone asks for "Double nine SIRENSESTER," do they say languidly: "Oh, you mean Double nine SISSETER?" And when they hear "Double nine SISSETER," do they drawl back: "Oh, you mean Double nine SIRENSESTER?" Anyway, when next I have occasion to ring up my Gloucestershire friends I shall ask for "Double nine CirENcester," with the accent on the second syllable, and see what happens to that.

* * * * * *

"This yer Spring weather be almost too much fer I,"

remarked my old dairyman this morning. Of course he was referring to the sudden warmth which has bathed the countryside during the last few days, but I say the same for an entirely different reason. This lovely Spring weather appears to have gone to the heads of both editors and agents, so much so that they all are yearning for articles on Spring, and, as usual, they all want them immediately, if not sooner.

During the past week I wrote three of these, and this morning, Sunday, was forced to cancel a perfectly good four-ball game of golf in order to write another, which was promised to be in London first post to-morrow. What in the world I shall be able to write about in April I cannot think, for already I have exhausted Spring. In fact, if anybody else wires for an article on Spring I shall blow up. Still, you never know—I have seen snow in April. However, this afternoon I went for a ride with Pam. Ostensibly we were on pleasure bent, but I must confess that I was studying the countryside very carefully just in case another editor of my acquaintance should go all Spring-like at short notice. I have a frugal mind.

We rode up through Grovely Wood. At every season of the year this wood is beautiful, but just now it is very lovely indeed. Spring's sudden visit seemed to have caught even the trees unawares, and they are hurrying to catch up with her, or, to put it in another way, Spring is positively bustling them into their clothes. As we rode I noticed that fresh colour was showing everywhere against the sombre black of their winter nakedness. Green predominated, but the beeches were covered with a pinkish film ; here and there a drift of almond-coloured palm showed against a background of dark-green spruce ; while around us on every side green honeysuckle twined eagerly amongst the breaking hazel buds.

But the loveliest thing of all was the continuous chorus of

the birds. When we entered the wood a pigeon or two clattered noisily away, a blackbird rattled his danger signal, and a jay screamed a hoarse warning of our intrusion. But when we arrived in the middle of the wood we stopped for a few moments to listen, and all around us was song in praise of Spring, sung by an invisible choir—coos, chuckles, chirrupings, baritone from the blackbird, contralto from the thrush, and every now and again a thin treble thread of melody from the smaller songbirds.

At long last my back has yielded to this riding treatment, so this afternoon we rode for six miles through the wood to a place where we had seen a black rabbit a week ago. On the way I told Pam that rabbits did not travel about much, and that most likely we should see the black one in the same spot. For once Fate was on the side of the elderly prophet, and Blacky skipped across the ride at the identical place.

Then came almost tragedy. Up till now our ride had been perfect. Pam had jumped two logs successfully, and her father had been gloating over the absence of aches and pains. But many other people had been tempted up into the wood by the glory of the day, and were enjoying themselves picking primroses. As we were cantering along the broad drive a lady in a red dress leading two black dogs appeared suddenly from the wall of hazel at the side, whereupon my old horse propped and shied violently across the ride. I looked round to see Toby copying his example, and Pam parting company with him. I pulled up with my heart in my mouth. What should I say to her mother? But I need not have worried. She scrambled to her feet, saying: "I'm all right, Daddy. Where's Toby?"

Toby had merely trotted a few yards along the ride and was standing there wondering just what was going to happen next. He was gentleman enough to allow us to catch him without much trouble, and soon we were on our way home. Once again I must confess that children beat me. Pam was much more concerned with the slur on her horsemanship than with her bruises, so I comforted her by assuring her that her father had only just managed to stay on. Thank goodness she does not know just how true that was.

However, I drew the line at further jumping on the road home. I had had enough shocks for one afternoon, and was anxious to deliver my child to her mother all in one piece. To all whom it may concern—the sight of a little heap of yellow jumper on the grass is not a pleasant one.

* * * * * *

To-day is quarter-day, and we celebrated it on this farm by shifting the dairy herd and all their traps from the downs to the valley, and turning the cows out into the water-meadows. This necessitated leading the bull for a half-mile along the highway, and, as usual, he objected violently. It occurs to me that I am getting to the age when a man cannot deal with refractory bulls efficiently, for this morning William nearly beat us, and I was dragged by him along the road in most ignominious fashion. The trouble is that he runs free for six months and does not take kindly to being put on a stick. Still, after this morning's training he will behave better in future; at least I hope so, for a bout with him every morning will be too much for me.

To-day I was forced to read the riot act to the boys in the neighbourhood. They do not seem to be able to understand that grass is a crop, and that now the pastures are being laid up for hay they must keep out of them. And for that matter, grown-ups are just as bad. Consequently, I shall be very unpopular hereabouts for a week or so, for I do not pay the rent of this farm for amusement, but in order to make the land show a profit; and to accomplish this my farm must have privacy during the growing season.

Yesterday evening I was called to the 'phone to take a telegram which requested me to write yet another article on this lovely Spring weather. Of course I replied that I would do so, and deliver to time, which meant that I sat up at my desk until three in the morning. Never, never have I worked so hard at anything. I had already written all and more than I knew concerning Spring, and I was fed up with that charming damsel. Almost I hated her, but somehow or other the job got done. It is amazing what one can do when both pride and need are the driving forces. But from now on I am through with Spring, and to-day I got as far away from her as possible. I went with my wife to a furniture sale in the morning, and to the pictures in the afternoon; and in the evening I drove into the club in Salisbury for bridge.

Usually it is pain and grief to me to accompany my wife to furniture sales, but this morning I enjoyed myself. I was not responsible for anything, so I smoked in peace and teased her unmercifully. She is very brave in her bidding for anything up to a pound, but after that her courage fails her. However, to-day she had a field day, buying copper scuttles, candlesticks, and other various small items, including elephants.

These last were the *pièce de résistance*, so to speak. The auctioneer's man, a huge fellow in a green baize apron, came in with five ebony elephants with ivory tusks and toe-nails on a tray, whereupon my wife said: "Oh! I've wanted elephants ever since I've been married." A cry from the heart like that I could not withstand. What a skunk am I, I thought, to deny my wife elephants for sixteen years! So I proceeded to make amends, and told her to buy them, and that I would stand the racket. Accordingly she and an Anglo-Indian colonel fought each other in shilling bids from five shillings to seventeen, at which price the hammer fell and my wife attained her heart's desire.

Further good husbandry at the pictures in the afternoon and the enormous win of ninepence at bridge in the evening concluded a most satisfactory day in which Spring was entirely forgotten. To-morrow is the last day of March, thank heaven! He has been a good month and a good friend to me, but I shall be glad to see the back of him, for there is no spring left in me.

April

In these days one of the leading topics seems to be traffic regulations, so it was a pleasant change last night to hear a friend revolt at this monopoly of conversation, and say : " Look here. I'm tired of all this talk about cars, and signs, and speed limits. Let's have a change. Does anybody here know anything about travelling ' Ride and Tye ' ? My father used to go to school like that, and I myself have travelled by that method many times."

Needless to say nobody knew what he was talking about, so we begged him to explain. Apparently this was the method of travel used by two people when they had only one horse between them. Supposing a horse travelled at twelve miles per hour and a man walked at four miles per hour, it was possible for both men and the horse to arrive simultaneously at the end of a twelve-mile journey in two hours.

From what I could understand, it works out something like this. The twelve miles are blocked out in two-mile stages. Rider and walker start together. In ten minutes the rider covers two miles. He dismounts, ties up the horse, and walks on. In that ten minutes the walker has trudged only one-third of the first two miles, and it takes him another twenty minutes to reach the horse ; by which time the other walker has walked two-thirds of the second two miles. Ten minutes later the first walker, now mounted, reaches the end of the second two miles, and so, on foot, does the first rider. Thus both cover the first four miles in forty minutes. Now the first rider mounts again, the first walker trudges on, and the four-mile procedure is repeated twice in the remaining eight miles, thus bringing both men and the horse to the end of their twelve-mile journey in two hours.

All that sounds more like one of the sums of my youth than a logical explanation, so for posterity's sake I had better draw a chart. From what I can see, none of the modern generation are interested in travel at such a slow speed as six miles per hour, so it will be well to leave an illustrated record of this method in order that they may realise what joys modern invention has taken from them. Besides, in all my ordinary writing I never get a chance to draw anything, and my bridge is too bad for me to dare to draw that familiar square and the hands of A, B, X and Y, with which the experts have such fun.

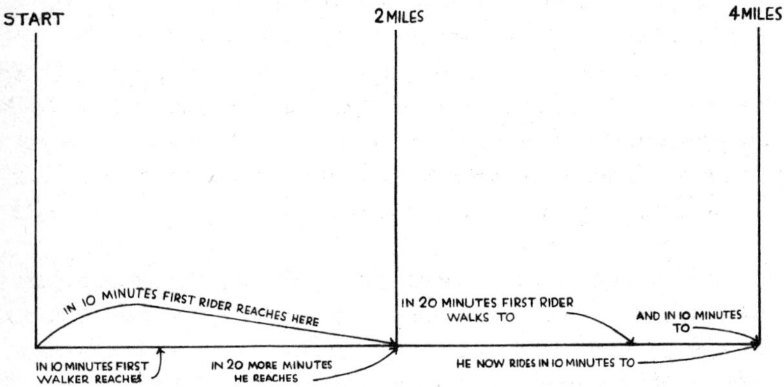

Of course, in these days this sounds a very antiquated, slow, and inefficient form of travel, but it had its points. For instance, it gave both travellers time to think; it enabled them to enjoy the beauty of the countryside through which they travelled; it provided suitable rest for horse and men; the hard work of the journey was equally shared; and, when contrasted with the present mode of conveying rural children to school, it wins hands down.

Other times, other manners, I grant, and to-day modern life demands that country children shall be transported swiftly in a mechanical juggernaut from their homes to their school in order that they may be fresh to assimilate the benefits of modern education. But riding a horse or a pony is a partnership from which any child is bound to learn much useful knowledge which cannot be found in text books. And when two children were forced to share one mount at " Ride and Tye " this threefold partnership taught even more.

The spelling of the word " Tye " is that given to me by my friend, who said that such was the only way he had ever seen it spelt. I should imagine that when this method of transport was in general use our word "Tie" was spelt with a "y," for it is a long time ago since anyone travelled in this fashion.

One more note. In case any modern should sneer at " Ride and Tye " as being inefficient, consider just how efficient it was. Supposing the tied horse got loose when both men were walking. There was always one man behind him and one in front. This old custom left precious little to chance.

* * * * * *

My, but the countryside is getting green, even though the wind has gone back to the east and rain is badly needed. I came back from town this afternoon by an afternoon train, so I was able to get a good look at Surrey, Hants, and Wilts.

I cannot help thinking that a long daylight train journey must be infinitely more interesting to a countryman than to a city dweller. Of course, at this season the swiftly passing pageant of the Spring scenery must be interesting to both, but when Winter comes and the landscape is bleak and barren, I imagine that the townsman must find his newspaper more entertaining than the view from the carriage window.

But at every season of the year the true countryman glues his nose to the pane and criticises the farming as it flows past him like a moving picture. Why? Just because he knows all the

a few minutes after twelve

actors, all the props, and the reason why this or that scene is being played. In effect, he is seeing his own life portrayed upon a screen. Such knowledge is denied to the city man, who must find his daytime train journeys tedious in consequence.

I feel quite sure about this, for once when a farmer friend was in a train a fellow traveller asked him the time. He replied immediately: "A few minutes after twelve." Whereupon his companion said in wonderment: "Excuse me, but just how do you know that? You've been looking out of the window for the past half-hour, and you did not trouble to look at your watch." "Well," he replied, "the carters in a field which we've just passed were putting the nose-bags on their horses, and they always stop for dinner at twelve o'clock in this district." At which explanation the townsman marvelled the more.

But this afternoon I noticed something which I did not find altogether pleasing. In several fields of spring corn which were showing green I saw gaps of unsown ground, where the tractor drill had been forced to turn too short in its circumnavigation of the field. From each corner of the field to the middle were crescent-shaped patches of brown earth showing against the green of the crop, and these gaps seemed to spoil the picture.

They reminded me of the tidy farming of my youth, and I wondered what my father and his foreman would have said could they have seen such a sight. Verily, I believe that my father would have pulled the communication-cord and sought out the culprit responsible for such slovenliness. But to-day I am conscious that such so-called slovenliness is not bad farming, but rather an honest attempt on the part of the farmer to make his farming pay. Tidiness does not pay, and the day of tidy farming seems to be gone for ever. In my boyhood the main object of both master and man was to farm well; now both have been forced to consider money as their main object, and as a result many of the niceties of farming have had to be discarded. No more does one hear the foreman or head carter say to his master: "Now, zur, doan't 'ee do it. Lookeezee, 'tis hrong." Now right or wrong does not matter, and instead one hears: "'Twunt pay to do thic, zo let ut goo." Such is the new morality of farming which modern conditions have forced upon the industry.

Of course Nature, with her usual tidiness, will do her best to cover up these sins of omission, and in a month or two those gaps in the cornfields will be scarcely noticeable to the eyes of the critic in the passing train. But next September those crescent-shaped patches of brown earth will show in the stubble as patches of weeds, and every true countryman who travels that route will mourn the days when English farming had its proper pride.

Pride, I know, is considered one of the seven deadly sins, but proper pride in good farming is surely a virtue. But to-day such a virtue does not bring its own or any reward, and in a world which reckons everything in terms of money, the farmer must fall into line or suffer. Even so, I must quote my father's old foreman once again, and say: " 'Tis hrong." Without proper pride in good husbandry farming ceases to be a worth-while life for a man, and, instead, degenerates into a sordid business. May I live to see the day when mankind puts money in its proper place and restores good farming to its honoured position in our national life.

* * * * * *

The Pigs Marketing Board has been so much in the public eye of late that a remark passed by a neighbour to-day concerning the outstanding financial success of a certain small-holder in his district is interesting. I have long known that " pigs is pigs," but never have I had the truth of this so forcibly illustrated. Wishing to impress upon me that this small-holder had made his money by reason of his singleness of purpose, my friend said: " You see, he kept his eye on the goal. Take his pigs. Why, he worshipped them. I tell you, his idea of beauty was a sow with a good trip of pigs; and his idea of more beauty was two sows with two trips. In fact, his life was based on a pig standard." One can hardly expect an artist to appreciate such a standard of beauty, but it is the only kind which will serve the man who wishes to succeed in farming from a humble beginning.

Some few weeks ago I preached a similar doctrine in an article in a farming paper, in which I stressed the need for hard work, thrift, and tenacity of purpose in the young farmer. The other day I noticed that someone had called me over the coals for such heresy, but still I am unrepentant, and to-day brought me a letter which contained the approval of another farmer. Which shows that you cannot please everybody and that it is waste of time to try to do so. This letter also contained a jingle which was new to me, but which did seem to point the moral.

> "Man to the plough,
> Girl to the cow,
> Boy to the barn,
> Wife sew and darn,
> And your rent is soon netted.
>
> Man tally-ho,
> Girl piano,
> Boy Greek and Latin,
> Wife silk and satin,
> And you'll soon be gazetted."

* * * * * *

This morning we had a snowstorm, just to remind us that Summer has not yet arrived, and that there is still a sting in Winter's tail. But I am not grumbling, for we have had two or three good wet days, and the weather is still decidedly unsettled, thanks be. It is at this season of the year that I am always greatly concerned whether I am the only fool in the country or the only wise man. My irreverent household and my ribald friends tell me not to worry, because at every season I merit the former title, but I have enough sense to take a considerable discount from their estimate. As one of my friends put it to me some years ago when we were talking of some local chaff: "You don't bother to rag folk you don't like. You let 'em severely alone."

Still, this year I think I can claim to be a member of a very wise minority of people who have rejoiced in the recent rains. For two long dusty years now rain has been conspicuous by its absence, and on All Fools' Day a week or so ago the parched condition of the countryside so worried me that I spoke aloud my desire for rain to all and sundry. As a result, I have come to the conclusion that I am the only person, in this district anyway, who likes rain.

My wife, the maid, and the dairyman's wife told me firmly that no woman ever wanted rain on a Monday because it was washing day. A Salisbury friend in the outfitting business replied to my spoken desire for rain: " We never want any rain in this business. It keeps people indoors and prevents them from buying our goods. And on a Tuesday, market day, rain is a calamity."

Later on, while I was getting my hair cut, knowing the barber to be an enthusiastic gardener out of business hours, I yearned audibly for rain, thinking that he would be sure to agree with me. Not a bit of it. He did concede that some rain would do a lot of good, but he did not want any rain on Wednesday, because that was his weekly half-day off.

During the evening I discovered that rain on the Thursday would be unpopular with my pupil because he had arranged to attend the last meet of the season on that day. In desperation I suggested that we might have a little rain on Friday, only to be told by my small daughter that such a happening would blight her young life almost irretrievably, because she was going to a Pony Club Paper-chase on that day. After that I gave up. Rain on a Saturday or Sunday I well knew to be a calamity in the eyes of the majority, as the English week-end is dedicated to outdoor sports and pleasures.

And that's that. On no day of the week is rain ever welcomed, and, apparently, in a properly regulated world, rain would fall only between twelve midnight and six in the morning.

But for once the Clerk of the Weather proved to be on the side of the fool or the wise man, whichever way you care to look at it, and we have had a lovely rain. Real wet rain, not just a shower, but rain for several days. Naturally I exulted openly and my glee has been a cause of offence to many of my friends. Almost I was chucked out of my club in town for remarking "Gorgeous weather!" while the rain streamed down the windows of the cardroom one afternoon. One man said that I should be put away into a lunatic asylum, and another demanded that I should pay for a new umbrella which he had been compelled to purchase that morning. Apparently he had not needed an umbrella for two years, and yet how he grumbled! And when I told him that I had never possessed an umbrella, he gave me up as an uncivilised peasant from the backwoods.

But why should I bother with an umbrella? I like rain. I like the good it does to everybody, I like the feel of it upon my face, and even when it soaks through my clothes to my skin. Consequently I have revelled in the recent April rains, for rain in April or May is to me, and should be to everybody, undiluted joy. For April and May are the months when growth is made, and too often they are cold and barren and dry. Rain at this season ensures a bulk of produce of all sorts from the land. Give us rain now, and we shall be content for the townsman to bask in brilliant sunshine during the remainder of the Summer, what time that same sunshine is maturing the growth which a wet April and May makes certain.

But that, of course, is merely the farmer's point of view, and, as I read in a Sunday paper only last week, who cares a hoot for farmers, anyway? Very well. To blazes with farmers then, and let us think of the townsfolk. They do not want rain on any day in the week at any season of the year. If they had their wishes granted, what would happen to them? Without rain, in spite of all their mechanical devices, they would go thirsty, and then in less than two hours the thin veneer of their civilisation would disappear. Even the thought of a thirsty London appals one.

So let us thank Providence that the ordering of such a valuable thing as rain is not in the hands of any government, dictator, capitalistic business, or co-operative company, and that it is not in human power to control it. Both town and country require a sufficiency of rain, and when it comes at this season of the year it does the maximum of good to all parties. No man who wishes for rain in April deserves the title of April Fool.

* * * * * *

This evening a very stiff and tired man sits at his desk. If he possessed any sense at all he would have gone to bed when his household retired, but pride, silly pride, keeps him up long enough to scribble something of the day's doings in his notebook.

For to-day I have been hunting for the first time since the Spring of 1921, and such an event should surely be recorded. The final meet this season was almost at my back door, so to speak, and the first cover to be drawn was almost on my farm. Such an opportunity was too good to miss in Pam's eyes, and so her old father tried to renew his youth. We did not get a decent run, it is true, but for my part I had a full day. My first responsibility was the safety of my daughter, and my second was the safety of myself, for in my own eyes I have a certain value.

In actual fact, the second responsibility proved to be the more onerous, for Peter decided to renew his youth also. He took one look at the hounds, cocked his ears, and his motto during the remainder of the day was " Let's go." So we bucketed about in a large wood from eleven until three-thirty, when the continuance of steady rain since about two o'clock made the father decide to chuck it, ostensibly on the grounds of his child's welfare, but in reality because he was dog-tired and wet through.

But never shall I forget the joy shining in Pam's face when we had a short burst of music from the pack, nor her obviously fit condition as we hacked home in the pouring rain. Toby behaved throughout the day like a perfect gentleman, while Peter was a decidedly naughty boy. There is no doubt that Doctor Toby has done Pam more good than any other medical man, for which he has my grateful thanks.

And now to bed—glorious bed!

* * * * * *

Good Friday has always been a general holiday on farms in this district, but yesterday I was at work. Some time ago I was asked to write "A Conversation in a Train" for the B.B.C., and it was broadcast late on Good Friday night. Consequently, I travelled up to town yesterday afternoon to take one of the parts.

London is a queer place. Although it was Good Friday, there were many workmen in the streets putting up decorations for the coming Jubilee, and their slightest activity brought crowds of interested spectators. Even to watch a man nail an imitation spear or even a flag to a pole, seemed to be all-absorbing to the passers-by.

But how varied modern life is! In the morning I was hacking through a Wiltshire wood, and soon after tea I was rehearsing in Broadcasting House. The broadcast was timed for ten-fifteen, and at a quarter to eleven I was walking down Regent Street wondering what to do with myself. London on a Good Friday night seemed to have few attractions, so I had some grub and caught the paper train from Waterloo, arriving home about three-thirty this morning.

And to-day I have done very little. I was tired, and sufficient for the day seemed the goodness thereof. So I have just lazed and smoked and revelled in the bursts of Spring sunshine which have been intermingled with April showers. Also, I have been thinking about that broadcast. Apparently it passed muster all right, and it has whetted my appetite. It played for twenty minutes, all dialogue, of course. Almost I have decided to try my novice hand at a play. But I don't know anything about play-writing or of the workings of the theatre, so I suppose my play will not get any further than just this thinking about it. Still, if ever I do manage to write one, this entry will be interesting, for undoubtedly this short broadcast conversation will be the reason for the attempt.

* * * * * *

Easter Sunday, and for my part another lovely, lazy day, during which I have been thinking of the Easter holiday, and that to the town Easter spells " Exodus," and to the countryside " Invasion." It is the first outdoor holiday of the year, and from time immemorial the leisure which it has brought to a winter-worn townspeople has been spent by them in visiting the countryside. Surely this is one of the finest examples of the correct use of leisure ? To-day we have more leisure, and to-day so many more people visit the country at Eastertide that the word " Invasion " is a fitting description of their coming.

For this great boon to an industrial people let us give credit where credit is due, and thank the recent improvement in mechanical transport of all kinds. By bus, by car, by train, by cycle, and by Shanks's mare, the Easter invasion of the countryside by the legions of pavement people is carried out. Some lucky folk can rusticate for four precious restful days, and even the poorest can manage to make at least one of the two Bank Holidays a day of green and perfect peace.

But will they do so ? Some will, no doubt, but many will not. The trouble is that a life lived in town amidst noise and crowds tends to make the liver unsuited to the country. Its loneliness and quiet seem to overawe him and make him uncomfortable. In consequence, he is rather apt to spend his country visit in close company with other visitors, and to take his gramophone or portable wireless with him in order to make a familiar noise when the strange hush of his surroundings becomes too much for him.

All of which is not so much the town-dweller's fault as his misfortune. For the English countryside is not a spectacle to be enjoyed by a crowd. At this season it is a wide expanse of varied charm, but its most exquisite beauties can be discovered by one or at most two persons only; for a crowd always destroys natural beauty by the mere fact of finding it. So if you would enjoy your Easter holiday to the full, even though you must make the journey from town as a unit of a crowd, choose only one companion for your ramblings once you have arrived at your destination, and get away from the crowd as quickly as you can.

Then, as soon as the mellowed fields and lanes of England grant you the privacy you seek, go slowly. One may hurry along a pavement, one may even commit that crowning folly of running up the tube escalator, but on holiday in the country one should dawdle—or, rather, meander. No other pace is fitting. You are in search of that comforting draught of country mixture which is brewed at Eastertide; and the countryside treats no hustler to this sovereign remedy for the ills which modernity has brought to mankind. Here is the recipe for it. Take so much time leaning on a gate and watching cattle grazing; lie down for a while and smell the good earth and the growing grass; stand for a few moments on a high down and gaze your fill on the patchwork quilt of England; visit the cloistered peace of a large wood in which the noise and bustle of your daily life will seem very far away; add just a small bunch of wild flowers to taste; and be grateful to the feathered choir around you for their melody. And there you have it, a country mixture which will do the winter-worn town-dweller more good than gallons of medicine.

But you have done all that so many times at Easter? You want to see something fresh? Very well! You come from rows and rows of buildings. Why not have a look at a different form of architecture? Sit quietly near a pond or a river, or even a puddle, and watch the master builders at work. There you will see the birds gathering the materials for the framework of their homes and also the mud which they use as cement. Watch how they try every inch of each straw or twig with their beaks before they pick it up and fly away with it. They do this to be sure that they can bend it, for anything too stiff for them to bend would be useless for their purpose.

Now go and find one of their finished products. Again, you should go quietly in case by the noise of your coming you disturb a sitting bird. When you find an untenanted nest, examine it closely, and you will marvel at the cunning craftsmanship it displays. Then think for a moment of two things. Firstly, of the many scientific and mechanical aids which man uses in building his nest; and secondly, that the builder of this nest has one tool only—a beak. If, after noting this, you destroy a bird's nest or steal his wife's eggs, you are past praying for. Go back to your town of brick and stone and cement and leave the countryside to those who can appreciate its marvels.

But what of the real countryfolk? How do they spend the Easter holiday? Many of them do just the same as they do during every week in the year—they serve the land. It is their job in life, a job which takes little count of Bank Holidays, and those who perform it so well and so patiently are literally the salt of the earth. Still, during recent years more leisure has come to the country, and to-day quite a large proportion of countryfolk manage to make holiday at Easter. Some of these use the same mechanical transport which brings the townsman to the country to enable them to visit the town, on the lines of one man's meat being another man's poison; but the majority attend the one rural revel which takes place at this season, the local point-to-point.

Here is the one occasion during the Easter holiday when town and country meet in common cause; for every type of country dweller attends it. The butcher, the baker, the farmer, the postman, the doctor, the squire, the lawyer, the labourer, the poacher, rich and poor, married and single, men, women and children, church and chapel, tory and socialist, the love of racing and the liking for a mild gamble which are inherent in most English people bring all these countryfolk and their town cousins together.

So at Easter the countryside caters for all tastes and for all pockets. Both the town visitor and the country dweller can enjoy their leisure either in a crowd or in peaceful solitude. But no matter what their choice, they will be in the fresh air of England's green—so very green this Easter—and pleasant land; for the Easter holiday is a country holiday to most of us.

This Easter, in spite of the catchy weather, there is a record invasion of townsfolk, so large as to be almost a menace to the countryside. But this need not be. The invaders will obtain great good and great pleasure from their holiday. A little care would enable them to make a pleasing feature of it that no country dweller will be compelled, when he looks around next Tuesday, to misquote a popular advertisement and say: "That's a lovely place, that was."

* * * * * *

This morning I bestirred myself to a little activity on the Bank Holiday, and went for a long ride with Pam, during which I received proof of the invasion of the countryside by townsfolk.

The wood, to use a Wiltshireism, "wur fair diggled wi' 'em," and so we explored its uttermost parts in search of privacy.

We were rewarded by the close sight of a wild deer, which jumped out of a wire-netted enclosure within twenty yards of us. Unfortunately it did not allow for the single strand of barbed wire which ran about eight inches above the netting, and so came a purler. However, no great damage was done apparently, for it picked itself up and vanished down the track at full speed.

Then came the contrast. A few hundred yards further on we came upon a town friend who was sampling Wiltshire's Easter mixture with evident enjoyment. First a deer, and then a London stockbroker! Both running wild in a wood, and both, in spite of the deer's tumble, revelling in the gorgeous weather and the wood's beauty. England is indeed a wonderful country.

* * * * * *

There is nothing much doing in the farming line which calls for comment. From now until haymaking we just keep on day after day milking the cows and doing odd jobs—chiefly fencing, repairing the damage of the past winter. To-day I showed my pupil another trick which the average farmer makes his car play when necessary.

We were taking down about a quarter-mile of fence and re-erecting it with new posts. When the time came to strain the wire, I tied a piece of rope to the axle of my car, and to the other end of this tied a finger from a grass mower. The shape of this finger enables it to hold against the barbs in the wire anywhere, and when you have the wire fixed all you have to do is to ease up in first gear until the wire is tight—you can break it if you are not careful—pull on the hand brake, and staple up the wire at your leisure.

I can remember reading a poem somewhere about the coming

of the wire fence to Western Canada. " Your barbs have pricked the bubble that was romance in the West," is a line which sticks in my memory. Truly, in recent years barbed wire has done much the same for our Wiltshire countryside, and has certainly restricted hunting possibilities. My farm now is a veritable birdcage.

And how much more difficult it is to put up used barbed wire than new stuff! To-day its barbs have pricked something more tangible than romance—namely, the hands of those engaged in erecting my fencing. Still, to-day most farmers would be badly off without barbed wire. Not only does it make a good fence to keep stock in, but also it makes the best fence to keep people out, and in these times the latter is the more important function of most farm fences.

This evening I sat down to rough out a broadcast talk on the Wiltshire dialect, and I must confess that I found it difficult. I am no scholar, and therefore I cannot talk learnedly about the derivation of dialect or of its historical origin. So I shall content myself with stressing its descriptive quality, and by talking a considerable amount of my native tongue. Few people like to eat meat without salt, and our general speech, owing to the spread of education and broadcasting, has lost much of its savour. There is such a sameness about it, a tiredness is possibly the better word; and most of us, when we revolt against this, instead of using good old English dialect words and expressions, try to infuse the wanted kick into our speech by the importation of American slang.

I have actually heard a lad reply to my dairyman, who had given him an order in broad dialect, " O.K., chief! " After that, I do not think a little broad Wiltshire over the microphone will come amiss.

* * * * * *

One of the reasons why so many folk hate rain nowadays is that in this regimented age the pavement dweller, either in a large city or in a provincial town, has almost forgotten that the source of almost everything which he uses, consumes, or enjoys, is the land. To-day he is just a unit of a vast crowd, all of whom are hurrying and bustling in a mechanical maelstrom. Consequently, he has no time to think, and tends more and more to take his ideas second-hand from the newspapers or the wireless.

In contrast, the countryman, by virtue of his comparative isolation and the slower speed of his daily life, has time to think; and, although to many he may appear a trifle slow in the uptake, his ideas are none the less sound. For they are his own ideas, which he has acquired at first hand from the careful study of something which has been running continuously ever since the world began. For instance, the countryman knows, no matter what the papers print or the broadcaster says, that the grass won't grow unless the rain comes, that if the rain does come the grass will grow and nobody can stop it, and that if the grass does not grow at this season neither town nor countryside can prosper.

To-day, the last day of April, drowner Jim came to me and said: "You niver knowed sich a wonnerful April in all your life, an' neether did I, an' I be nigh on thirty years older than thee." Needless to say, I agreed with him. Day after day during this bounteous month I have spent my leisure in walking and riding and gloating over the beauty and promise of the Wessex countryside. A smiling landscape, England's green and pleasant land in literal truth. A countryside which seems to grow greener every minute as I gaze upon it from the top of the downs. A land of down and valley and stream, under all of which lies solid chalk. A countryside which, thanks be, has not changed very much during my lifetime. A land of cows and sheep and plough and pasture and grey churches and thatched cottages. A countryside which, thanks to April's rains, is full of promise of abundance. The land in which I was born and bred. The England I love best.

Golly! But I am becoming as lyrical as a Spring poet! Such flowery language is hardly suited to a farmer's notebook. Yet why not? Rain, blessed rain, is to blame for that burst of lyricism, and why should I be ashamed of giving thanks so openly? Too often April refuses to weep, suffering the outrage of the bitter blast of March in barren dry-eyed grief. But this year she has wept and smiled through her tears in wholly delightful fashion. I, for one, hope that her sister May will copy her example.

a land which will not change very much

May

This morning I went to Wilton Fair, the smallest May fair in my memory. Ever since the general adoption of motor-transport of livestock these old fairs have been becoming steadily smaller, and, of course, the weekly markets correspondingly larger; but the exceptionally small amount of sheep and cattle in to-day's fair was the result of foot-and-mouth disease restrictions. I talked with a Dorset farmer who told me that he did not think he would ever get the smell of the burning animals in his district out of his nostrils. " It's there when you go to bed," he said, " and it's there when you wake up, and the whole district fair stinks." Still, he seemed to think the present method of fighting this disease to be the best one, although, like all farmers, he hated the very idea of destroying apparently healthy animals wholesale.

Apart from this the atmosphere of the fair was a fairly cheerful one. April's good rains have brought on a wealth of grass keep, and therefore mouths to eat it were at a premium. A temporary rise in price of any farm product because of natural causes may bring a little chaff between farmers here and there, but, even so, the old-time gusto seems to have disappeared from farming. My father and his contemporaries ragged each other at fairs and markets because they knew, not only that they were financially secure, but also that they would most likely continue in the same condition. To-day few farmers can say either with any real belief, and the conviction that whatever happens the countryside will be sacrificed to the towns seems to have settled on the farming world with the same depressing effect as the smoke from the foot-and-mouth fires over the Dorset countryside.

But there is always one thing which cheers me—whatever happens, the land will remain. I said that to a friend in town the other day, and he exclaimed: " The land will remain. What a line! What a title! You ought to do something with that." How it annoys one when words which are spoken from the heart are treated by the listener as a clever remark! Often I try to be clever—after all, a writer cannot write foolishness all the time—but when one talks or writes of something for which one cares deeply, the desire to be clever cannot be present.

So, as I say, it is the permanence of the land of England which cheers me in these days; and, even so, I fear for the future of our countryside. The best I can foresee for it—and this I fear will be the worst possible fate—is that it will be preserved as a playground for our town population. Better a poorly paid servant than a kept woman. Still, maybe the future will bring about a return of the land's one-time importance, for, to repeat, when the existing population of this island are dead and buried in the land, the land will remain.

* * * * * *

To most people May would not be a sporting month, but to the countryman there is no month that does not bring its particular form of sport. This morning, just when I was in the midst of dealing with a pile of correspondence, I received a message that one of the water-keepers wished to see me. No correspondence is as important as my relationship with friends of this type, and so I deserted my desk to commune with him.

Like all countrymen he came straight to the point. " 'Tis a fine sunny day wi' no wind to speak about," he said, " an' I be gwaine to try to wire a vew pike. Knowin' as you do enjoy thic caper, I jist called to tell 'ee as you'd be very welcome."

Was ever invitation given in more pleasing fashion? I certainly do enjoy "thic caper," and I realised also that such an invitation was worth much fine gold. "Give me ten minutes, Walter," I begged, "and I'll be with you. Here! you have a glass of beer and a cigarette, while I make my excuses to my secretary." "Thank 'ee kindly," he replied, adding, "but you ain't got to ask nobody's permission, 'ave 'ee?"

How true it is that one half the world does not know how the other half lives! Walter looks upon me as a wealthy man who can please himself how he spends the day. I should not be surprised but what he envies me. And he is paid to wire pike—think of it!—and I have to obey agents and publishers and secretaries and the public in order to earn my livelihood.

I returned to the study and polished off the letters post haste. "I'll sign 'em this evening," I told my long-suffering secretary. "If anyone rings up to-day, tell 'em I'm away from home on business. I'm off pike-wiring with the water-keeper."

"But you can't," she replied. "There's this and that and the other which we promised to get off this week, and to-day's Friday."

"And to-day's pike-wiring as far as I'm concerned," I retorted. "You stay here and tell lies over the telephone like a good girl and I'll bring you back a six-pounder." And with that I bolted. It was the only way, for my secretary is a conscientious individual, and I knew better than to argue with her, or, for that matter, with any woman. For most of the year I am but a toad under the various harrows of a wife, a daughter, a secretary, and an agent, all of one sex; but even a toad must escape occasionally.

Ten minutes later Walter and I were in the water-meadows, safe from women and men and machinery. Each armed with a slender hazel wand with a wire noose at its tip, we strolled slowly along either side of the river bank. The river was gin clear and without a ripple, and in a few minutes Walter pointed to a pike. It was out of my reach so I watched his artistry. Gently his wand slid beneath the water, and I watched it slowly advancing towards the pike, which lay like a piece of dead stick nearly half-way across the stream. Inch by inch it slid forward until it was a foot or so upstream of the pike, and then very slowly it drifted downstream. Then, suddenly, the pike disappeared in a spray of silver drops, and in a few minutes it reposed safely in Walter's haversack.

Soon after came my turn. An eight-pounder lay motionless in mid-stream. Walter could not reach him, and at my first effort the noose drifted past him, merely scraping his side with its outside curve. At the risk of a wetting I leaned outwards at full stretch, and just managed to get it over his head. The moment when my noose was drifting down towards the first fins was excitement at its best. Then I heaved and the fish was out on the bank, snapping his jaws ferociously.

In this fashion we meandered upstream with varying success until my tummy insisted on food. Then we adjourned to a nearby pub, where at darts Walter and the landlord beat the local thatcher and I very badly. After lunch we worked back down the tail stream, which gave us another half-dozen pike, and I wandered in to tea with two beauties dangling from a withy over my shoulder. No one could call such fishing artistic, but I defy anyone, even my stern secretary, to say that a day spent in this fashion is waste of time. For as a result I worked like a trojan at my desk from six until midnight. I must tell her to-morrow that the earliest rotation of all was rest and crop, and that the only improvement we have been able to make in it since time out of mind has been change of crops.

* * * * * *

This morning I received a letter from a farmer in the Midlands asking me whether the car-sweep was an economical method of harvesting hay. I replied that in these days if I were forced to wagon hay I should not make any, mainly because my temper would not stand such a slow method. I mentioned this to a friend this evening, who said: " If that feller only knew it, that letter's worth fifty quid to him this coming haymaking; that is, of course, if he've got sense enough to act on it."

" You know," he went on, " you'm quite right about temper. Mine just won't stand hosses nowadays. They were all right years ago. Haymaking's always a rotten job, but then, even if we didn't want to do it, we had the ships, we had the men, an' we had the money too. Now I've got one hoss on four hundred acres, precious few men, an' no money at all."

When one thinks of the old-time haymaking scene with the enormous loads of hay trundling towards the rick like galleons in full sail, the swarm of men engaged, and the financial security of farming at that date, his simile seems to be a very apt one. The ships, the men, and the money too—nowadays there's nothing of that left to farming. But, even so, the fight goes on.

* * * * * *

Although it was a trifle colder to-day the weather has been so glorious that all the fruit trees have suddenly come into blossom. So pleasing is the drift of snow against the green in every cottage garden that I hanker to get away to a fruit district—either to Evesham, Pershore, or Kent—and have a look at the orchards in all their beauty. But I cannot manage it this season, worse luck. Why? Simply because I cannot spare the time, that precious commodity which is my sole stock-in-trade and of which I have far too little. Always nowadays I seem to be toiling uphill trying to catch up with my work and never succeeding. Somehow I have a notion that this state of things points out either laziness or incompetence on my part. The man who is boss of his job always has time for anything, so my slave-driven condition means that my job is boss of me. Well, there are worse taskmasters.

So to-night I must shake out the wings of thought and let them carry my mind to the fruit blossom while my body sits here at my desk. Now where shall I go? To Kent, I think, to see the cherry orchards. Pershore and Evesham I saw last year, but it is three years since I saw the Kent cherry trees hung with snow.

For that pleasure I am indebted to a farmer friend, who invited me for just the right week-end to see the blossom at its best. True, I know that he had another purpose in mind—to demonstrate to a Wiltshireman that the Kentish farmer knew his job—and in this he succeeded. I admired his farming, his business acumen, his organisation, and, above all, his personal energy. In fact, so dynamic was he that I felt a poor weak robin by comparison.

He had over a thousand acres of Kent devoted to intensive fruit and vegetable production, comprising several small farms dotted all over the fruit district. If my memory does not fail me, he had three hundred acres of strawberries that season. Obviously he was a wealthy man, but how he worked, and how he played! Always at full speed, by car, or on foot, for I cannot remember ever seeing him walk—he trotted most of the time, and in moments of urgency ran like a boy. After he had shown me all his farming, on the last evening of my visit he asked me how I should improve on his methods if I had the same land and the same capital invested in it. To my everlasting credit let it here be recorded that I answered honestly.

" You have some seventy thousand pounds invested in your farming," I said. " You have, for instance, three hundred acres of strawberries. You do the work of any three men now at blossom-time, so I presume at picking time it's the work of six ? "

He grinned and nodded.

" And you ask me to tell you what I should do in like case. Well, I'll tell you. If I had half that capital I should buy my strawberries from a barrow."

" Just what I've always thought," he chortled. " You Wiltshire farmers don't know what work is."

Which, of course, was a fair enough jibe, and I had asked for it, but somehow I think that a middle course between my indolence and his feverish toil is the best method of living. For why do I regret that my lazy habits have made it impossible for me to visit Kent again this year ? Not so much because I want to see his farming methods, but because I would like to see the blossom on his cherry trees once again.

But whenever and wherever I come across a successful farmer who is running a farming business of similar financial size I find this same intense personal toil. Apparently, in farming the success or failure of the enterprise, no matter how large it may be, depends largely upon one man ; whereas in other businesses the responsibility is shared by or delegated to several people. During my lifetime I have seen several limited liability companies start farming in a large way, and I have always seen their finish in comparative failure. Which shows, I suppose, that farming, despite the co-operative and planning and controlling ideas which are prevalent just now, is and must be an individualistic business no matter how large or small it may be.

* * * * * *

I knew it was too good to last. Until May came, from the countryman's point of view, the season was almost perfect. January was kindly, February brought rain in sufficient quantity, March dried the land and so enabled the farmer to sow his seed in a good tilth, and April brought warm rains the moment the sowing was finished. As a result, everything in the countryside, man, bird, beast, and plant, sat up and began to take notice; or, in other words, everything in both farm and garden was lovely.

On the rare occasions when this sort of thing occurs the countryman, born and bred, while he is grateful for such bounty and openly admits his gratitude, begins to worry. He does not know just how and when the blow will fall; but he does know that fall it must, or his life would become too easy to be borne. Well, this year May soon told him all he wanted to know.

She brought Winter back to chasten the countryside. Both frost and cold east wind she has used to put a brake on Spring, and in all her temper she does not seem to be woman enough to weep. Still, the countryside need not worry very much over her icy mood, for two reasons. Firstly, because her chilliness is unseasonable, and cannot last, for June will soon be here; and secondly, because the first four months of the year gave everything such a good start that the countryside can withstand May's cold with equanimity.

In spite of it the weald of Wessex is clothed in a green garment from the downs to the rivers. The grass still grows apace, and each day sees a new flower or tree in blossom. Granted, the east wind is doing no good, but it is not doing too much harm, and I think May might just as well make up her mind to behave, for she is playing a losing game. Still, I hope that when she repents (or should it be relents?) she will deign to weep copiously in regret for her unseasonable conduct.

Surely her unnatural marriage with December should be sufficient reason for tears?

* * * * * *

In his altogether delightful biography of Richard Jefferies Mr. Reginald Arkell makes the statement that farmers never fish. It takes a brave man to disagree with Mr. Arkell, for he has the gift of conveying reproof in rhyme in such a subtle but biting fashion that one hesitates to risk his displeasure. But in this instance I must do so. For, mark you, I am a farmer, and I not only fish, but I enjoy my fishing. Still, I will concede, generally speaking, that few farmers used to indulge in this form of country sport.

But to-day I find that the number of farmer-fishermen is rapidly increasing. I have been hunting around for the reason, and I have come to the conclusion that it is the desire for privacy which is responsible for this change in farmers' habits.

Some weeks ago I was asked to help in a broadcast programme in which about half a dozen men talked, each for five minutes, on their choice of spending a day's holiday at this season of the year. Fishing, climbing, hiking, bird-watching, sailing, and flying were amongst the chosen ways of holiday-making. There was no previous collaboration between the speakers, but I noticed that in every case the desire to get away from the crowd for one day was the ruling motive. Each man stressed that his perfect day's holiday must be spent alone or at most with but one companion. Apparently, although we all liked our fellow men and women, neither of us liked them in the mass; and the wish to avoid the crowd was very evident.

The trouble is that modern life forces most of us to spend our days in the midst of crowds. Physically we are bustled and jostled during both work and play, and mentally we are buffeted by other folks' ideas through the medium of the Press or the microphone during most of our waking moments. Even the farmer is now a mere unit in a vast national scheme of planning, and no longer can he stay on his land and just farm according to his own inclinations and in comparative privacy. To-day he must consider and worry over so many things which, although they may be connected with his farming, are definitely not on his farm, that it is no wonder during his scanty leisure he is becoming more and more attracted by the peaceful privacy of fishing.

Of course, so are many of his town cousins, with the result that fishing is becoming more and more expensive. Still, a few days' good fishing can be obtained by most farmers very cheaply if they know their way about—and most of them do, for otherwise they could not farm for long—and the wise farmer-fisherman lays the groundbait of courtesy in his rural swim during the winter months, so that the summer catch shall be heavier each succeeding year. A day from this friend, another from that, a complimentary ticket from a club for whose keepers the farmer has been able to perform some useful service of great value to them and of little expense to himself. A live-and-let-live mode of life in the country always brings its own reward—at least, such has been my experience.

Having succeeded in this the rest of the matter is not expensive. A second-hand rod can be purchased for a few shillings, half-a-sovereign for the licence, a small expenditure for flies and casts, a duster in one game pocket for the catch and one's lunch in the other, and the joy of the stream in summer time is yours.

Ah! what joy it is! Alone for one whole summer day. Alone in the water-meadows! No one can ring you up; no one can get at you by motor-car; five minutes after you have left the road you are lost in a green shady peace, safe from both

Five minutes after you have left the road

friend and enemy until night forces you to seek the haunts of men once again.

And not one dull moment will you have during that lovely, long, leisurely day. You have a rod, suitable flies, and there are fish in the stream, for you can see them; but all this does not mean that you will catch any. Fishing is not so simple as shooting—not by a long, long way. It is an art, and a very difficult art at that. You must pit your wits against those of the fish, and you will find him no mean opponent.

In order to outwit him you must concentrate to such an extent that all other worries will be forgotten. Instead of being a man you will become a fisherman, a being with but one desire—to succeed in catching a wily trout on a dry fly, a thing which looks so easy when it happens, but which is so infernally difficult to accomplish.

Whether you catch any fish or not you will be bound to succeed in one thing, and that is in spending a day of peaceful privacy in the most perfect setting in all the world, the water-meadows of England. I have yet to meet the man who can describe that as a wasted day, even for a farmer.

* * * * * *

Recently I have visited three large farmhouses, where in each case I noticed that the tennis court—one place boasted two of these—was not used. In pre-war and even in immediate post-war days such a thing would have been impossible, for then every farmhouse court was in constant use throughout the summer, and the standard of village tennis was a high one. Now, each succeeding summer sees more and more farmhouse courts falling into disuse, and, as far as I can see, this change in rural life will continue to take place. The reason is two-fold—the minor part because of bad times, and the major because of the coming of motor transport.

Tennis on one's own court means tennis parties, an expensive hobby and one which most farmers' wives were forced to give up soon after 1925; while those of the farming community who want good tennis and can still afford the necessary time to play it and the money to pay for it have discovered that they can obtain this more cheaply and of better quality at a club than on their own court.

The latter truth always obtained, but prior to the motor-car the tennis club could not compete with the home court. Then, the farmer entertained his friends on his own lawn, where rarely and then only by much skilful wangling did a well-matched four come together. Now, in a quarter of an hour he can be at the nearest club, where he will find good tennis, varied society, and no responsibility either for the condition of the courts or as a host; and all this for one tithe of what it would cost him to keep his own court in trim and to hold, say, three tennis parties during the summer.

Here is yet another change in rural life which has been caused by the coming of the motor-car, and there is no doubt that this invention should be blamed for the many plantains in the neglected farmhouse tennis court. Of course, many people would say that it was a change for the better, but when I look around at the young folk in this district I begin to wonder. I will admit that the new system gives them better tennis; but it robs them of something very valuable which the old system granted to the farmer's family. I mean the appreciation of friendship, for in my boyhood farmhouse tennis was much more than a mere game; and either as a guest or as a host it taught young folk not just how to behave, but how to wish to behave, a much more valuable quality.

* * * * * *

The first crop which a farmer cuts is wool, and May is the

Hand Shearing. The first crop a farmer cuts is Wool

season of its harvesting. I do not possess any sheep, but I made it my business the other day to visit two sheep-shearing gangs, one using hand shears and the other using machine.

I am no judge as to the quality of the work done, but it did appear to me that the machine made a better job than the hand shears. But in either case the result is not pretty, for there is something almost indecent about the look of a newly shorn sheep.

One thing I did discover was that many of the one-time hand shearers have gone over to the machine. Of course, no good craftsman is a fool, and I have always noticed that it is the indifferent workmen who moan the most about the coming of machinery to the farm. They realise that they themselves cannot stand up to such competition, while the first-class men know that they will always be wanted.

Still, there was one curious difference between these two gangs of shearers. The language of the machinists was definitely more lurid and more blasphemous than that of the hand workers. Was this due to the perversity of inanimate things, or to what?

* * * * * *

As a result of the recent dry years or possibly because of some unknown cause there seems to be a veritable plague of rabbits this summer. The other evening a friend took me for a drive over some of Wiltshire's wild country, during which we must have seen ten thousand rabbits, for the countryside was, as my friend put it, " fair twizzlin' wi' 'em."

In one place we came to a deserted field barn and two cottages, in one of which the head-carter of my boyhood was born. Now there is just the shell of the cottages remaining and enormous rabbit burrows take the place of the one-time vegetable gardens. It was indeed the abomination of desolation. I will admit that it was obviously poor land, and its name, Starveall Bottom, indicates that it was never the Land of Goshen. But years ago it did pay to farm; now it has been left to the rabbit.

I here offer a free plot to any writer who wishes to write a fantasy describing England after the next war when everybody in the world will have been gassed off. Up to date, although there have been several books of this type, no one has thought that in their burrows the rabbits would escape the gas. Within two years of the stoppage of civilisation I have an idea that rabbit-rule would be the most probable result of such a catastrophe, for in less than two years rabbits take charge of any tract of land in this country which man has abandoned as a bad job.

* * * * * *

Phew! I wish I had not written that May could not do much harm with her cold wind, and that she would only be helping Winter to fight a losing battle with Summer. I have never liked May because generally she is cold and unfriendly, but never before have I known her in such an icy mood. Snow, hail, wind, and frost have swept the countryside—not just a short storm or a mere one degree of frost, but a twenty-four-hour blizzard, and severe frost. This morning the early potatoes in the gardens were brown, but from the papers I see that other districts have suffered even more. Ross-on-Wye had fifteen degrees of frost, and Farnborough in Hampshire nineteen degrees. This must spell disaster to the fruit crop, for while most fruit can stand a few degrees of frost—cherries, for instance, can stand up to eight—double that figure means a catastrophe.

It just shows what a chancy business fruit-farming is, and that some years the fruit farmer needs to make a large profit in order to withstand losses such as this May frost has brought him this year. Still, although the papers tell me that the strawberry growers are ploughing in their crops as a total failure, I doubt whether this is true in very many cases. Nature has a wonderful compensating way with her, and usually the result of bad weather never turns out so badly as one expects. Consequently, in spite of this hard, damaging frost, I will bet money that there will be plenty of strawberries for sale in a month's time.

* * * * * *

The frost has gone, and occasional rainstorms sweep from down ridge to down ridge, blotting out the valleys between for five minutes at a time. But it is still cold, and neither indoors nor outdoors brings comfort. The one means facing an east wind, and the other means an unseasonable fire in the grate. Also, the continuance of this cold means little change on the farm.

Everything is marking time, and is going backwards in volume daily. So, Charlie told me this morning when I visited the bail, is the milk yield. Finding nothing to please me, I walked on to see if the sugar beet were up well enough to be flat-hoed. On the other side of the road near by I found old Jim busy hoeing a small patch of mangolds, which I put in for the sake of our three riding horses next winter. Funny how one's farming changes. Years ago when I milked forty cows on this farm I grew ten acres of mangolds for them. Now, when I milk eighty cows, I don't grow any mangolds for them. The reason is that having laid water on to every field it hardly seems worth while to grow and haul out to cows a root which contains about ninety per cent. of water.

Here and there I could find small sugar beet plants, but they seemed to have precious little life in them. Seeing that Jim would soon be out of a job, I called him to come over and have a look. He did so, and together we meandered over the field with our heads down, looking for all the world as though we were in search of treasure.

"They be there," said Jim, "but they be on'y jist there. They doan't grow, zno, an' they wun't as long as this yer cold weather do las'."

"Well, what about it, Jim?" I asked. "Can you see them well enough to flat-hoe them?"

"Ay, I 'low I kin pick 'em out. Lord, 'tis on'y vower acres. You lave I bide yer fer a week an' I'll git roun' the lot."

"Well," I said, "we shall have to pick up a hand or two directly for haymaking. Supposing I get 'em now, and send 'em up here?"

"Then I goos away, guvner," came the reply. "I doan't mind work, but I cain't stand zeein' they dole vellers messin' about. 'Sides, you doan't want to worry about yer 'ay. Ef zo be as we doan't git zum warm rain soonish, you wun't 'ave much more'n one rick to make. You lave I to thease yer vew beetroot, an' get 'ome a-writin' er else a-prayin' fer rain."

I obeyed, and left him to it, but on the way home I could not help thinking that the old workmen who have never been out of work would be far more harsh in their treatment of the unemployed than any committee of employers. Old Jim, I know, still holds to the doctrine of "He that does not work, neither shall he eat."

* * * * * *

I find that I read much less than I used to do. As a farmer-milkman I read on the average twelve library books every week; as a farmer-writer I scarce average one. Which seems queer, but what is still queerer is that more often than not I find myself reading old favourites, simply because they give me greater pleasure than the newer books.

This is a sign of old age. I am standing still, and letting time creep ahead of me. Indeed, I am fast becoming an anachronism in these times of change, for I find that I am one of the few middle-aged men hereabouts who is living in the house in which he was born. And I fancied myself such an adventurous blade as a young man, when I left for Canada at eighteen. Now my reactions to modern books tell me that I am in grave danger of becoming an intolerant, narrow-minded hayseed, for it is rare that one really interests me ; I read some of them, but a week afterwards I cannot remember anything of what I have read.

My critical attitude towards youth is yet another sign of age. I must do something about it. My dislike of crowds, coupled with the discovery that I could get a living in solitude without rubbing shoulders each and every day with all sorts and conditions of men, has led me into a rather self-satisfied groove, I fear. I must get out of it somehow. Living in one house all my life is perhaps praiseworthy, but letting my mind stay put in one place is to be deplored. Age has always mourned the inefficiency of youth, but, dash it, I don't feel so very old. At least, only when an east wind in May depresses me. No matter how many hours one spends at a desk, it is impossible to write of life unless one lives it in much broader a fashion than my present habit. Well, if this cold weather has been the cause of my discovering this failing of being self-satisfied and narrow-minded, I should be grateful to it.

* * * * * *

Ascension Day, and also the annual Club Day of a neighbouring village. Yesterday a friend of mine who has farmed there for many years told me that it always thundered on Ascension Day, and that it would thunder to-day. I looked at the sky, noticed the direction of the wind, and laughed at him. " There's no sign of rain," I said, " and you can't have thunder without rain. You're getting superstitious in your old age." " All right," he replied. " You wait and see, like Asquith."

To-day we have had a thunderstorm. I don't know why, and I still don't believe that there is thunder every Ascension Day, but I merely record the fact that my friend's prophecy proved to be correct. Of course, this evening he called, ostensibly to take my wife and me for a drive, but in reality to say " I told you so," a sentence which gives more pleasure to the speaker than any other in our language.

But I forgave him, for he told me a very interesting thing about village Club Days. Apparently years ago these and similar fêtes were the only occasions during the year when the farm labourers had a good square meal of meat, and some of them, he told me, used to suffer from meat-poisoning owing to the amount they consumed at these functions.

" Most folk don't know anything about those days," he said, " but I can tell you that the men had hardish doos then." (Whether the plural of " do " is " doos " or " does " I know not. The phonetic spelling must surely be " dooze.") " Only just enough grub to enable them to work, and meat only on Club Days or when they killed a pig. Nowadays the caterer for the Club Feast reckons on exactly a third of the meat per head that was consumed just before the war. The world gets better in spite of all we say sometimes to the contrary."

Which, of course, is true, especially of the English countryside, in which to-day there is no under-nourishment and precious little poverty in spite of the depression in farming. A comparison which gives proof of this is that while in my boyhood the agricultural labourer and his family were hard put to it to get enough bread, nowadays they spend more money in bus fares than in bread during every week of the year. In addition to the fact that man cannot live by bread alone, one must now add that he cannot live without petrol.

* * * * * *

It occurs to me that I have another grouse against May. All work and no play makes even the countryman a dull boy, so the other day I decided that it was high time my fishing-rod came out of its winter quarters. A chalk stream in May, what more can any dry-fly man desire?

Let me state definitely that in this May he can and will desire quite a lot more, chiefly, of course, a rise in temperature. To put it bluntly, there was nothing doing—no fly on the water, and no fish on the move. That trusty friend the March Brown, even when dropped like gossamer with consummate skill, failed to achieve even the slightest suspicion of a rise. All I caught was the beginnings of a superb cold. Realising that such a bag required careful cooking, I returned home and lit the fire; and, until the mayfly tell me that the weather is behaving, I shall do my angling from the depths of a comfortable armchair near by. There I shall fish the glorious stream of reminiscence, on which any fisherman can spend an hour when he wills.

Miss May, in spite of your early smile, I do not like you. How I hope that June will make amends for your disgraceful behaviour!

June

This evening I received yet another proof that I am rapidly getting old, or rather that I am an old man. I drove some twenty odd miles to a large public school in order to fulfil a long-standing promise to yarn to the boys about possible careers in farming. Prior to the talk I dined with the Head and two of his staff, to find to my horror that I was the oldest man present! Older than a head-master! Ye gods!

Fierce questioning afterwards by modern youth concerning farming matters made an interesting, pleasant evening, but I drove away about eleven o'clock feeling quite senile.

* * * * * *

In the wood above my farm there is a large patch of rhododendrons, and just now, a trifle late owing to the cold season, they are in full bloom. To get them to grow in this chalk country—rhododendrons just hate lime—some soil from the New Forest was carted to the site when they were planted. So, at great expense and after considerable toil and trouble, these lovely flowering shrubs now bloom each year on the top of a chalk hill for the delight of all who care to pass that way.

This morning, Sunday, thinking that their bloom was about due, Pam and I rode up to have a look at it. Coming away from the coloured bank of blossoms were a man and a woman. Her arms and his were filled with branches of blooms which they had ruthlessly torn from the bushes. Both robbers were well dressed and appeared to be decent, average English people. No, I'm wrong. The word " decent " should be omitted.

* * * * * *

What a wonderful writer Shakespeare was! One can quote him and misquote him quite aptly in connection with every phase of modern life, for generally his writings are as true to-day as when he wrote them. But on looking round the countryside at this season I always see something which is in direct contradiction to one of his most quoted lines.

To-day few people plant trees, but years ago many people planted them for the benefit and pleasure of those who came after them. So, when I look at the wonderful avenues and stately trees in this part of England during the leafy month of June, I think of the men who planted them, and say to myself, "The *good* they did lives after them."

* * * * * *

Having an hour to spare the other morning while we were up in town, my wife and I suddenly stumbled upon Berwick Market. I am very hazy about London streets, but if you wander two hundred yards down Shaftesbury Avenue from Piccadilly Circus and turn to the left you will find this place—the ordinary street market of fruit and fish stalls, etc., but the extraordinary street market of dresses and stockings and all sorts of ladies' garments.

And there, after his wife has made her choice of the goods displayed, the farmer can go horse-dealing with the salesmen to his heart's delight. Anyway I thoroughly enjoyed myself in this fashion. After a great barney with one man, he said, "Guvna, I admire your nerve. Yer wife's a lucky woman." As I say, it was for all the world like horse-dealing in Wilts.

But the great attraction which that market had for me was the cheerfulness of its people. Most of the businesses were family ones, I should imagine; and everybody was keen and interested in the possible customer. I daresay we were an obviously easy mark for them, but even now, when the enthusiasm of bargain-hunting has been forgotten, my wife is quite satisfied with her purchases. Any farmer's wife who would like to meet some real live people rather than the almost mechanical units in a vast business, should have a stroll through Berwick Market when she is next in town.

* * * * * *

The first week in June usually spells haymaking in Wiltshire, but this year, just as I was about to begin cutting grass, down came the rain, and it looks as though I shall have none cut for another week. Rummy how the weather alters things. A month or two back we were all talking about an early season, and now here we are, a good fortnight later than usual.

Ah well! No farmer can rule the weather, which is a good job, not only for him but for everybody. Still, it doesn't do for a farmer to let the weather rule him more than he can help; by which token I shall down sixty acres of grass next week, rain or shine.

There is a tide in farming at every season which must be taken at the flood, and especially does this apply to haymaking, although "at the right moment" should be substituted for "flood" in this connection. In other words, when grass is ripe enough to cut, cut it must be. I must admit that taking the tide of haymaking either at the "flood" or "at the right moment" will not lead to fortune in these days, but it may lead to some good hay; while a "wait and see" policy at this season leads nowhere save to disappointment and bad hay.

* * * * * *

It is cold and stormy and the weather is decidedly unsettled, but we made a start with the cutting to-day. A friend from town who came out into the field with me was greatly impressed with the work of a seven-foot power-drive mower coupled to a tractor, but he chaffed me about my conversation with Charlie, who was driving the outfit. "You fellows use tractors and all kinds of machinery in your farming," he said, "but you still make the weather your chief topic of conversation." "And why not?" I countered. "In spite of all our mechanical aids for dodging and fighting it, the weather still says 'Aye' or 'Nay' to all our plans. The methods of farming may change, but the essentials remain the same as ever."

To this he disagreed, saying that everything in the countryside had changed out of all knowledge since his boyhood. I still stuck to it that it was only the methods which had altered, whereupon he challenged me to give an illustration.

"Well," I said, "at this season of the year every night just before he went to bed my father used to go outside for a few moments, look carefully at the sky, and make an estimate of the morrow's weather. I switch on the wireless and listen to the weather forecast. The land's the same as ever; it's just the method of tending it which has changed."

He was still unconvinced, so I gave him another illustration, this time from a doctor's life, which did prove my point to his satisfaction. A young doctor once told me that his father always took some carrier pigeons with him in his trap while on his country rounds. When he needed a remedy urgently, he sent the prescription home by this means, and a lad then cycled out with the medicine as soon as the dispenser had made it up. Now his son drives a car instead of a horse, and uses the village telephone for urgent messages. Just a change of method, that's all; the essentials of life in rural England are still the same. But no one can deny that improved transport and communication have removed a deal of pain and terror from the lives of the inhabitants of outlying villages.

* * * * * *

Sixty acres of grass cut and rain and thunder day after day just to show one Wiltshire farmer that farming is not by any means under human control despite all the modern machinery at his disposal—such was the position at home and the best way of dealing with it seemed to be to run away from it, a thing which I promptly did.

This apparent cowardice was, in reality, taking advantage of my father's teaching and example. During haymaking and harvest, while the sun was shining he was a trial to everyone under his jurisdiction: but when the weather prevented his farming plans being carried out he proceeded to take a holiday. In other words, when it was possible to hustle on the farm, he saw to it that everybody did hustle, and at these times he used to come down on the more indolent section of his staff like the veritable wrath of God; but on a wet day in haymaking or harvest he was the cheeriest soul imaginable.

Which, to my mind, is not a bad example for any farmer to copy. To strive and worry and toil when any of these can aid one's farming is surely sound; but to do so when the weather conditions render them worse than useless is silly. Better far to run away from a scene which merely emphasises man's inability to conquer Nature. So, immediately after tea to-day my wife and I set out in the car in search of a change of scene for a day or two.

Some people say that soon there will be no countryside remaining, and that already the towns have spawned and spewed red brick and drab concrete over nearly all the acres of one-time beauty, but this is not so. There is still an English countryside remaining, before whose spacious grace the towns and cities seem quite small and oh! so tawdry. The downs with their short turf, golden gorse, skylarks, and rabbits are still here, together with the peaceful streams and narrow valleys which lie between their ridges. In spite of the modernisation and mechanisation of farming most of the country is still divided into little fields by stone walls or hedgerows. Elm and beech and oak and ash and poplar and many other trees still populate the scene. In the Lake District the mountain streams still chatter and sparkle; and in the flat shires the grass is still as green as of yore.

The first question to decide was which district we should visit, for there is still so much of England's beauty that we have not yet seen, and so much that we want to see before age makes travelling a task rather than a pleasure. We hankered after the lake district of Cumberland, but that was too far away for a short trip—after all, our Wiltshire haymaking would have to be tackled when the rain stopped—so we set out for Wales and its Marches, a district which was new to both of us.

Marlborough, Swindon, and Cirencester were fairly familiar ground, but after that two Moonrakers were exploring. Cirencester to Gloucester took us through some charming country; but, while my wife admired the stone walls and coveted the grey stone farmhouses, somehow I felt that there was not a very good living for a farmer in that country. I shall probably get into hot water for saying this, but there did not seem to be much "guts" in the Cotswold land; and I will wager that its farmers were glad to see the rain.

We reached Gloucester at seven-thirty. There are, I believe, nearly sixty thousand inhabitants in this city, but they must be very law-abiding, for we saw only one policeman there, and he was such a pink-cheeked stripling! Funny how young the police seem to be nowadays wherever you go. The reason is, of course, not that they are younger than of yore but that we are all much older. Still, pink cheeks must be a feature of the city of Gloucester, for my wife told me that all the girls had " that schoolgirl complexion." Anyway, Gloucester gave us a very good dinner, and in contented mood we drove on to Newent, where we stayed the night.

* * * * * *

There are a lot more nag horses around Newent than there are in my part of Wiltshire. I say that with certainty, although I never saw one of them. But I heard them. While I was lying in bed this morning they clop-clopped past the hotel—hauling milk to the station, I imagine. Their drivers must have taught them how to stand up on the tar, too, for they all went by at a great rate.

Breakfast was a feast. Our one fellow breakfaster had stayed at the hotel many times, and knew the country. Also, wise man, he had made good friends of some of the countrymen. Result—he had wangled enough freshly-picked mushrooms for all three of us. These having introduced us—and what better introduction could one wish ?—during the meal we talked of cabbages and kings.

Somewhere between these two divergent topics somebody mentioned golf. Immediately our companion's face lit up. He was a middle-aged, rotund little man, not at all the sort of man one would have suspected of a secret and all-absorbing passion to break eighty ; but from that moment Henry Cotton had nothing on him when it came to enthusiasm and real love for the Royal and Ancient game. He told us of courses on which he had played and of courses on which he hoped to play in the future. In effect, between mouthfuls he played golf with us. When his breakfast was finished he brushed the splendid curve of his waistcoat with his napkin, and sighed, " Yes, it's a great game. What a pity it is that business interferes with it ! " It was a cry from the heart.

Then he wished us good-bye and set off for his day's work.

I hope he did good business, for while he was not exactly an athlete in build, he was a great-hearted little sportsman, and I shall always remember him with pleasure, for his company was even better than his mushrooms, and they were first rate.

* * * * * *

Always when I go away from home I make a resolve to scribble out my impressions of each day before going to bed, and invariably I forget to do this. This Welsh trip has been no exception. I did write up the first day before we left Newent, but after that I did not set pencil to paper. So on this first evening at home I must make some sort of a record, for there has been no rain to-day and I hope haymaking will claim all my attention for the next week or so. Well, four days have I spent in Wales and its Marches, and the result is that I want to know why one hears so little of this part of our island. The lay of the Eastern Counties is and has been for years a continuous lament, so much so that the townsman must be forgiven if he considers them to be all England as regards farming; but no one apparently has ever heard of the Western Counties.

Disparity in size has certainly nothing to do with this, for a glance at the map showed me that the Western Counties, just Wales and its Marches leaving out the South-west, are if anything the bigger district. Quality of farming cannot be the reason, for in this respect the West has nothing to learn from the East, in spite of the more difficult contour of its landscape. In beauty and charm of countryside the West is an easy first, so I suppose it is the closer proximity to London which accounts for the strange and unwarranted importance of the Eastern Counties in the popular view. Things have changed little since Cobbett's day, for the Great Wen still rules the countryside which supports it. Still, I cannot help thinking what a great educational effect it would have on the farming communities of both East and West if they were able to visit each other's districts, and learn something of each other's advantages and disadvantages.

But the real reason why the West of this island is so very much the West and so rarely meets the North, South, or East, is the difference in the language. Wales is still Welsh-speaking Wales in many of its rural districts; and I, a Wiltshireman, would have found it well-nigh impossible to find out anything concerning Welsh farming had it not been for the good offices of a Hampshire friend and the courtesy of a friend of his. By these devious means I obtained an introduction to a Welsh land agent and auctioneer, who showed me round the Corwen district, and he, being able to speak both English and Welsh fluently, translated the Welsh farmers' gibberish to me, and my English gibberish to them. In this fashion my wife and I explored Welsh farming.

Naturally the bulk of it is devoted to livestock, for the amount of land which it is possible to plough (not by any means profitable to plough) is a very small proportion indeed, and even this is divided into such little fields. And over all the mountains frown. Mainly, of course, the farming is sheep-farming, corn-growing playing a very minor part, obviously because neither the land nor the climate is suited to it. I talked with one farmer—incidentally the only one who talked English—who was renting a mixed farm of just over a hundred acres, and he told me and showed me that he had only about twelve acres of grain, principally oats. His predecessor had, he said, let the farm down badly by putting nearly half of it into grain every year. "Yess indeed," he said, "it wass shameful. And it did not pay. No! Why, he sold his grain. Bad farming, yess indeed. I feed all mine, yess, and buy more. So the land gets better. That iss why I have mostly oats. They are so

a Welsh mountain farm

dear to buy. Too dear. We need them cheap, yess." But that farmer, mark you, was paying a much higher rent for his little awkwardly-shaped fields than is customary in many parts of England where the fields are flat and much more convenient for farming of any type.

The majority of farms in North Wales are even smaller than his, but most of them have attached to them a run on the mountain for so many sheep, which, of course, is a valuable asset. Each small flock has its particular ear-mark, as there may be many different flocks running on the same mountain during the summer. One farmer—his christian name was Roderick—invited us indoors to inspect the book of ear-marks. This was printed from cover to cover in Welsh, and a sight of it made me feel that I was indeed in a foreign country. I asked our guide and mentor whether there were many folk who spoke only Welsh, and he told us that in some places he was forced to sell as an auctioneer in the native tongue; while our host, who I think by this time had decided that we were safe to talk to, told me in halting English that there were still some Welsh villagers who had never seen a railway train.

Of course, the background of all the Welsh farming is the mountain run for the sheep, and consequently every farmer has at least one good sheep-dog. This particular district is the home of the well-trained Welsh sheep-dog, and one of the local farmers had won the Championship cup for Britain. We only saw a dog performing the ordinary duties necessary when driving a small flock down a lane, through a gate, and other simple things, but it was enough to show us that the dog understood every word and wave of the hand from his master. Indeed, one could well imagine that the animal thought out the business for itself.

The Welsh sheep has existed on the Welsh mountains and

hills from time immemorial, but during recent years the breed has been much improved; but the improved and therefore larger sheep are to be found only where the pasturage is of better quality and the fields are enclosed. Where the mountain is common pasture to several farms it is obvious that it is difficult to effect much improvement in the sheep.

But from the sheep I saw I do not see much need for improvement. Granted they are small, but the large joint has been long out of fashion. They are hardy, their meat is of first-class quality, and they are suited to the country. That last is a great point in their favour. Not only can they live well where our south country hurdled sheep would starve, but they can graze quite safely over very rough country. It was a common sight to see a ewe and lamb standing on a rock and eagerly nibbling the grass at its edge in such a place on the side of a mountain where one false step would have meant a swift roll for at least a quarter of a mile. Incidentally, these mountain rangers during the summer months know that the grass in the valleys is of better quality than that on the mountain, and so always they try to work downhill. Consequently, every farmer who goes up to the mountain to have a look at his sheep gives his own and any others he may find a good " scoush " uphill.

Compared with the average farm buildings in this part of Wales ours in Wiltshire are positively palatial, but I found that most Welsh steadings housed some fine stock. From what was in my eyes a dark hovel our friend Roderick led out a topping pedigree bull, whereat my wife let me down badly by beating a hasty retreat. This bull was a champion from the Penrith country, and I afterwards found that all the stock on this small Welsh farm—sheep, cattle, horses, and pigs—were well bred; and it was evident that the system of Government premium sires for all classes of stock is doing good work.

There is no doubt at all in my mind that the Welsh farmer is a worker, and that he deserves all he gets and more from his labour. Indeed, sport and pleasure for the farmers in this district were conspicuous by their absence. We saw no tennis courts, and no village cricket, but, as I say, we saw a dickens of a lot of work being done—at least by the natives. The visitor comes to Wales for sport, and during our stay the salmon fishing in the silver Dee was at its best. I saw one fisherman catch an eighteen-pounder, which whetted my angling appetite. The salmon fishing was all let, but I found that a day's trout fishing was easy to come by. Accordingly, having one free afternoon and evening, I took my rod and went to try my luck.

On the Wylye I am used to a thirteen-inch limit for trout, but my ticket told me that on the Dee the limit was only seven and a half inches. I started fishing a Greenwell's Glory down stream in fast-running water, and in a few minutes I had hooked something. When I got my fish over the net I found he was a bare six inches; and then, to crown all, a salmon nearly three feet long leaped out of the water within three yards of me! It was too much, and needless to say I soon returned my tiddler to his native element with strict instructions to hurry up and grow. I caught half a dozen more of the same size, but I have yet to catch a takeable fish in Wales.

Unfortunately it rained every day during our tour, and my wife said that she imagined it always did rain in Wales because she had seen more umbrellas in four days than she saw in Wiltshire in twelve months. Which, now I come to think about it, was true enough. Everybody in Wales has an umbrella, and few people ever go out of doors without carrying one. It has suddenly occurred to me that the only umbrella which I have ever possessed is a golf umbrella. I suppose it is the

The Silver Dee

presence of so many mountains which tends to bring rain. Everywhere we drove the slate-blue crags frowned over such little green fields and such sparkling, rushing rivers. The clouds clustered round the mountain top, and then perhaps for half an hour the rain would blot out the valley. And even when the sun was shining by the silver river where the salmon were leaping, high above a steady drizzle draped the mountain and silver streaks of running water decorated its flanks.

Still, in spite of the rain the Welsh countryside has a peculiar charm. The valleys are green and peaceful and unspoilt, and every now and again as we drove through them we obtained peeps of exquisite beauty. But one can have too much of a good thing, and two Moonrakers soon had more than their fill of eternal mountains. Our road home lay through Bettws-y-Coed, Bangor, Carnarvon, Dolgelly, Newtown, Builth Wells, and Abergavenny to Ross and Gloucester once again. But long before we reached England we were sick and tired of mountains and rain and white cottages with slate roofs, and longed for a sight of our friendly downs and cosy thatch. Such scenery is not so majestic as the Welsh variety and possibly not so beautiful, but it is definitely more welcoming and kindly.

But I am glad that we made this trip, for one result of it is that I am much more contented with my farm in Wilts. I liked Wales well enough but I should not choose to farm there, for the Welsh farmer works very hard for very little, and I am a lazy dog. But I will readily take my hat off to him for so doing. He is a better man than I am—yess, indeed, whatever.

* * * * * *

To-day was hot and sunny, very hot, and so we began to pull the hay up out of the swath where it had almost grown in during the past wet week. It was damaged, but not absolutely spoilt. Still, it was in such a state that even the most modern swath-turner and side-rake could not make much of a job. Still, we got one field ready for carrying next day. But it was hard work, both for machines, men, and horses.

It occurs to me that one effect of the increased use of mechanical transport on a farm is that the few remaining horses have become of less value per horse than they were years ago. The trouble is that the odd horse or two which one now keeps do not do much if any regular hard work like ploughing, and in consequence they cannot do a decent day's work on the rare occasions when circumstances demand it. Or perhaps it is that few farmers nowadays take any pride in keeping good young horses; or again that one only wants some real work from the horse when the weather is hot and the days are long.

Anyway, the torrid heat to-day proved to me that my horses—how I longed for some of those good horses I saw in Wales—could not deal with a light horse-rake or swath-turner for very long in the heat of the day; and in consequence I have had a draw-bar fitted to the sweep-car and to the milk-van. There is that about machinery—it doesn't get tired.

Still, against that advantage there is the undoubted superiority of the horse over the machine in that the animal rarely breaks down and refuses to move at any speed whatsoever. And machinery does possess this very annoying habit—I who have just suffered from a bout of it can speak with authority. For one whole sweltering day I went from broken-down car to broken-down tractor and thence to broken-down side-rake. Not bad break-downs, but little trivial things which no one could have foreseen or prevented. But I must confess that by the end of that day I was not an easy person to cross. Still, everything has been buzzing along happily since, and my temper is fast returning to normal. It is curious how the perversity of an inanimate machine can raise a man's worst passions.

* * * * * *

At this season of the year this district has always been filled with the scent of hay, and nowadays, owing to the increase of pasture land, this is intensified ten-fold. This evening, in order to save time, I drove through some twenty miles of Wilts in order to pick up a spare part for a haysweep, and the countryside fairly stank of hay, and everywhere haymaking was in full swing.

More and more is this becoming a mechanical job in Wiltshire. Old cars of every make imaginable, including to my knowledge one Rolls-Royce, were pulling rakes and swath-turners and mowers, pushing haysweeps, and working mechanical stackers. Tractors were stuttering in every field, busy at similar tasks. Wiltshire was getting in its winter fodder, working at high pressure against time and sun and possible rain. Of course, to the townsman haymaking must still seem to be a rather charming, leisurely business, for from the top of a hill or even from the roadside the urgency and almost frantic hustle of the work does not obtrude in such a spacious setting. I pulled up my car in one place which gave me a wide view, and the scene appeared quite peaceful. Far below me a car pushing a sweep was travelling about the field in a cloud of dust and steam, while I could see a steady stream of hay passing up the elevator at the rickside. I took the trouble to time that car. In brought in three loads in ten minutes, and in the same time those three loads were pitched into the elevator by somebody. And it was hot and thundery and the stout fly was busy. Possibly from that range a non-haymaker would call it a pleasant, peaceful scene, but I who am a haymaker of some experience thought of the sweat and toil and frantic haste which was going on. The machine enables the work to be done with fewer men, but those remaining have to work harder than their forebears.

Having wasted a quarter of an hour in this fashion I hurried home, and after supper fitted the new part to the sweep satisfactorily, so, given a fine day, we shall be at full speed again to-morrow.

* * * * * *

This evening, owing to a thunderstorm just after tea, I was able to sit down to my desk quite early. During the past few days it has been half-past eight before I have got in from the hayfield to supper, and when I have tried to jot down a few lines I have discovered that physical tiredness, while it undoubtedly leads to mental content, is not conducive to much scribbling.

When the rain came on to-day the rick-maker was moved to grouse at the weather and to say, " I niver knowed it more caddlin'." Until this moment I always thought " caddling " to be a Wiltshire dialect word, but I have just discovered the word " caddle " in my dictionary, the meaning given being disorder or confusion or disturbance. And a sudden thunderstorm in June when you have got a field of good hay in the process of being picked up is just that.

Still, I do not think we should ever grumble at our climate, for, in spite of its tendency to be " caddlin'," it takes a lot of beating. If one can forget one's hay for a moment—and in wet weather one might just as well do that as to worry about it—one must admit that the English countryside is lovely during summer, even when it rains. That country lane with its puddles, its dripping trees and hedgerows, the birds piping, and the smell of everything around you growing and revelling in the rain. It occurs to me that only in England can one find pleasant wet; and here in high summer the whole world seems to be loving it and lipping with it. And when the storm is over and the sun begins to shine, how the countryside sparkles and laughs on both sides of the road !

Most by-roads and lanes are tarred nowadays, so to the credit of the motor-car we must place the fact that our roadside hedges are not covered with dust in dry weather ; but against that we must set the loss of that indescribable scene, that of a dusty English lane in hot midsummer—green and dust and honeysuckle and sweet briar, and still more dust and the feel of the sun on the back of one's neck—lovely. On which cheerful note I will go to bed, for to-morrow is July, from whom I crave one boon, just four fine, sunny days in the first week to enable me to break the back of this year's hay harvest.

July

Just now I have a young lad of eighteen staying with me. He is going into the Air Force, and from what I could gather his chief, almost his sole, reading has been papers such as the *Autocar* and *Flight*. Anyway, his one obsession seems to be speed, and my careful motoring at a steady forty miles per hour on straight roads filled him with barely-concealed scorn. He was very bitter in his comments on the thirty-mile speed limit in built-up areas, mentioning one piece of road near his home, some eight miles, which, he said, should be decontrolled. " Why ? " I asked. " The houses are not continuous," he replied. " And just look at the waste of time. It takes me five minutes longer to do that journey now." But when I asked him what he would do with that five minutes if the limit were lifted he had no answer, and he looked at me as though he considered me quite crazy.

Which, of course, I probably am, but what in the world is the good of saving five minutes unless they are to be used for some worth-while purpose ? Anyway, I told him that a vote on this question would result in a huge majority in favour of the limit at present in force ; and that even the majority of motorists would vote for its continuance. And when he asked me rather scornfully on what I based the latter statement, I pointed out to him that quite a number of motorists have little children.

* * * * * *

July is giving us perfect haymaking weather, and everywhere farmers are taking full advantage of it. To-day I pressed my budding airman into service, partly for a good farming reason that his help would expedite matters a trifle, and partly, I confess it, from sheer malice aforethought. Horses, either to ride or to drive, were too antiquated a power for him, so I put him on a tractor for one long sweltering day. Just think of his feelings the while! Four miles an hour uphill, downhill, and along the level. A governed engine, and no means whereby the driver could either increase or decrease the vehicle's speed. Occasional stops to oil the heavy double seven-feet swath-turner which the machine was towing, and over all the hot, workmanlike sun of July. I was very careful to see that he did not drive a car that evening after supper, for as a relief from that steady four miles per hour on the tractor he would have broken all speed records and most probably his neck also. Which would have been a pity, for, as modern youth goes in an old hayseed's opinion, this lad is a deal better than the average, both in common sense and in manners.

Incidentally, if anyone is at all dissatisfied with the running of a car, here is the cure. For one long day drive an old car pushing a haysweep or a tractor coupled to a power-drive mower. Then, immediately you knock off, get into your despised private car and drive slowly and carefully home. It will run like a Rolls, noiselessly, and its value in your mind will be enhanced by at least 100 per cent. On the lines of the punishment fitting the crime a day compulsorily spent in like fashion would have a most salutary effect on the exceeders of the existing speed limit. And having written that I would almost bet money that before long I shall be caught and fined for that very particular crime, for the modern car slips past thirty before one is aware of it.

* * * * * *

July, hot July with a vengeance, is doing us proud, and apparently does not know how to be "caddlin'." For which relief much thanks. Already the back of this season's haymaking is broken, and the winter oats are beginning to don a harvest tint. Which means that owing to the rain in June we farmers are all behind with our work, and shall not get our customary breathing space this month, but shall be forced to jump straight from haymaking into harvest. Still, we must not grumble, for there is an abundance of hay. Indeed, one of my neighbours put it like this to-day. "There's hay everywhere," he said. "Finished haymakin'? I tell you we shan't finish before October." Which, of course, means that next winter's keep is assured. I am in like case, for the pastures and meadows in which the cows have been grazing must now be trimmed. Mainly for the sake of tidiness, for here and there and everywhere the thistles show; and in a minor degree for hay, for most of the trimmings will be worth the raking.

Talking of thistles in July reminds me of an old rhyme which my father's old foreman used to quote. It went something like this:

"Cut a thistle in May,
Labour flung away.
Cut him in June,
Come again soon.
Cut him in July,
And he's sure to die."

And that, I think, is correct.

* * * * * *

For my sins I have been forced to spend two torrid days in London, and I have just returned home to Wiltshire and the fag end of haymaking feeling much more contented with my lot. We farmers are often tempted to make rather a lot of capital out of the fact that we have to work outdoors in all winds and weathers. From what I saw of some of my very good friends in town during this hot weather I have decided that it is far worse to be compelled to work indoors and to be unable to get outside until work is over for the day. Just now my London friends have my deep sympathy, for London this week, either indoors or out, will not bear description.

This evening Charlie, my dairyman, foreman, and general factotum, asked me if there was any need for the men to work overtime after tea while gathering in the trimmings of the grazed pastures. " They've had about a gutful of workin' till eight this weather," he said. Naturally I told him that they could please themselves—overtime rates for harvesting trimmings would not pay me—but I could not help thinking what an illustration of the farm labourer's better standard of living this incident provided. Years ago they were anxious to earn extra money at overtime, simply because their regular weekly wage did not provide sufficient for their needs. Now their wage does do this, and in consequence they will only work overtime when in their eyes the land's needs require it. And good luck to them. Years ago they had a poorish deal, and even if the pendulum of time has swung definitely in their favour and a trifle against the farmer, one cannot grumble. It was due to them.

* * * * * *

And still the sun shines daily from before breakfast until after supper, and still the rural world is haymaking. Part of my business in London having been the purchase of a good second-hand car, and my own haymaking being finished, this morning seemed to be a good chance to try out the new bus and at the same time to have a peep at the doings of my western neighbours. Accordingly Pam and I made a circular tour of Wilts, Somerset, and Dorset.

There was hay everywhere

Wiltshire is practically through with haying, but the other two counties, especially Somerset, were hard at it. In her small fields the tractor mower and motor-car haysweep are not so popular, and the hayloader and the wagon were very much in evidence. Always this district is a trifle later than Wilts with its haymaking, and this year it has a bumper crop. There was hay everywhere, and knowing that the practice on these rather small farms is to haul it along the road to the farm buildings I drove carefully. Even the best of second-hand cars cannot deal very successfully with a load of hay, and this morning there seemed to be one of these trundling along round every bend.

In the afternoon we all attended a pony gymkhana in a neighbouring village. Great fun. Competitors and ponies of all shapes, sizes, ages, dispositions, and capabilities. What hopes were dashed this afternoon! For many of the ponies it was the first time out in public, and, as one maiden of thirteen said to me with tears in her eyes, " Sandy jumps beautifully at home, but here he just won't. Oh, I'm so cross with him."

And Sandy just wouldn't jump, in spite of the good horsemanship of his owner, who literally made him do the round although he refused several times and knocked down the obstacle more often than not. In the double she had my deepest sympathy. Sandy jumped the first hurdle and bluntly refused the second, and there was my lady pounded amidst the laughter of the crowd. It was too much, and I said a quiet " Good lass " to myself when her whip descended on Sandy's rump with all the force of her arm and the venom of her disappointment behind it.

Somehow I don't think that Sandy was used to such treatment at her hands, for he bundled out of that double in double-quick time, fled the wall like a Leicestershire hunter, made light of the triple bar, and finished the round perfectly. And later on he made amends by winning the potato race for his mistress in fine style.

Pam, of course, missed no detail of the proceedings, and has decided to enter the lists herself at the next gymkhana in the district. This evening her beloved Toby was taken out into the paddock, and serious practice for the potato race took place. Like most girls, she is more keen on riding than most boys. Which, I suppose, is as it should be. Women have always lagged behind men in most things, and nowadays the modern boy is playing with motor-bikes and aeroplanes while his sister is satisfied with riding a pony, a pastime which filled the bill for her grandfather when he was her age.

There was a great crowd at to-day's gymkhana, which once again proved to me that English village life will never pass away, no matter what inventions come along to upset its even tenor. When the car and bus first came to rural districts village fêtes and junketings fell out of popular favour for a while. By these new means of transport everybody went into the towns for their fun. Now the wheel has turned full circle, and village fêtes are more popular than before. This afternoon the riding ring was surrounded with motor-cars, directions to the competitors were given by means of a loudspeaker, and in the intervals music was broadcast.

But the fête was held in the same park where it had been held since time out of mind; a descendant of the old squire had given gracious permission; descendants of the pigeons which a hundred years ago had cooed from the leafy depths of the tall trees near by cooed on the same soft note to-day, and the July sun bathed the whole scene as of old. The whole business proved to me once again that England's rural life remains unaltered in essentials by modern invention, simply and solely because it is rooted deeply in that one wholly permanent thing, the land.

* * * * * *

In England rural sport of any kind is often, too often, a rather serious business. Most people who engage in it feel it incumbent on them to wear the correct clothes, to use the correct gear, to speak the correct language, and to play the game according to the unwritten book of country life. Which, of course, is as it should be, for, like contract bridge, sport without any conventions would be impossible. But sometimes I think that the sporting occasions from which I have obtained the most enjoyment have been those distinguished in my memory by their almost total lack of obedience to any rule or convention. This afternoon's fishing expedition provides a good illustration.

Pam, three of her friends of the same age, and I set off for an afternoon on the lake. I took my fly rod just in case, and during the drive down assured my passengers that the boathouse contained at least four rods suitable for perch fishing; for this was the object of the trip. We loaded up the punt with tea and rods and bait and ourselves, and then I rowed steadily out to a suitable spot, where we anchored. In due time I had four worms on four lines, four floats in the water, and four little girls quivering with excitement as they held their rods. At this point the unpaid boatman lit his pipe.

For another ten minutes nothing happened, which rather damped the enthusiasm; but before this had entirely waned one float bobbed out of sight, and its owner squealed with excitement. "Ooh! I've got one. What do I do now?" I gave the necessary instructions, and then, just as I was netting a perch of about six ounces, another fisherman let out a yell, and then another, and then another. Perch are like that. When they do, they all do.

From that moment the boatman was busy. Perch are awkward things to unhook, excited little girls are rather apt to fall overboard, I was the only person present who would put a worm on a hook, and I was very conscious that we were floating over ten feet of water with a muddy bottom. However, by working hard, shouting advice and caution, and perhaps through the mercy of a beneficent Providence, I managed to untangle crossed lines, unhook the fish, and rebait without losing a passenger.

During the next two hours we caught about three dozen, and then the perch slacked off, so we had a riotous tea. If I had eaten half what my companions averaged I should have suggested a sleep, but apparently repletion has an opposite effect on little girls. Having demonstrated that they could catch perch they yearned for something new. Could they explore the lake? Could they—great applause at this suggestion—could they row me to any part where I might catch a trout? Of course they could. So after having tidied up the interior of the punt a trifle, feminine youth and beauty double-banked the oars, while middle-aged masculinity sat in the prow and tied on a blue upright.

My crew's efforts undoubtedly caused the punt to move, but its course was definitely an erratic one. They will need considerable coaching before they enter for public competition. Still, amidst much effort, more laughing, and advice from everyone present, the punt zigzagged up the lake to the shallow end, where basking trout can sometimes be coaxed to take a dry fly. This part of the lake lies above a low bridge, so low that both crew and passenger had to lie flat in the bottom of the punt to make the passage. This accomplished, I stood up and prepared for action, beseeching my crew to go very slowly, and if possible, straightly. Slowness is very necessary at this dry-fly game on a lake. Your first cast at a likely fish is generally a long one. The next is obviously much shorter ; and, unless the punt is barely moving, before you know where you are it is passing right over the fish.

There is no doubt that I was very lucky this evening. Usually when you have spectators you cannot catch any fish, and I am certain that my crew had little faith in my blue upright, no matter how much I swished it about. Anyway, five minutes after we had shot the bridge I was well stuck into a three-pounder, and yelled to my crew to stop rowing. They obeyed, and immediately crowded up to my end of the punt to watch the fun.

A three-pounder in several acres of clear water is no easy proposition to handle, and what with seeing that he did not make a dive at the punt and snap off by getting underneath it, and trying to keep both eye and a hand on the more excitable members of my crew who were in imminent danger of a bath at any moment as they fought for the landing net, life was very full for the next five minutes. But a three-pounder is a three-pounder, and could not be lost through feminine squabbles, so I chose the lady for the landing net, and yelled to the other three to sit down. Three times I had my fish almost over the net and three times he rushed away, but at last I got him right over it, and a flushed damsel scooped him into the punt amidst loud applause.

Everybody voted this type of fishing to be great fun, so we pushed gently up the lake for another half-hour, missing several trout, but catching one more. When we reached the top end, where a small stream runs into the lake under another bridge, I was prepared to call it a day, and lit another pipe, but my companions wanted to see if they could get the punt under that bridge. I gave the necessary permission, and amidst much splashing we edged towards it. Underneath it we got stuck, and then one of my ladies yelled that she could see a trout lying near the wall. She grabbed the landing net and leaned outwards. I grabbed her legs in case of accidents, and then the miracle happened. She broke all the rules of fishing behaviour and of fishing luck, for somehow or other she got a foot-long trout into the net, and shied him into the midst of her companions, giving them a complete shower bath as she did so.

That, as far as I was concerned, was definitely that ; and as time was getting on and I was responsible to three sorrowing mothers, I said that I would row home the mile to the boathouse. As a special favour I permitted four worms to be trailed behind the punt, and this resulted in three more perch during the journey. Then we all piled into the car, and soon I deposited my companions at their several homes ; each with a dish of fish, and each determined to cook them whatever parents might say. But when I got home I discovered two things. First that I was dog-tired ; and second, that I could not remember ever having enjoyed a fishing expedition more.

I don't quite know what my trout from that lake cost me during a season. Somewhere about five shillings a pound at least I should think ; but they are dirt cheap, simply and solely because of the peace and beauty and privacy of that lake and its surroundings. Those three things are hard to come by in these days, and whether I catch any fish or not I never regret an afternoon or evening spent in that old unwieldy punt. Tall trees stand by the lake's edge ; swan, wild duck, moorhens, and many other varieties of wildfowl swim upon its surface ; in certain places cattle and horses come down to drink ; there is not a house to be seen ; and in sunshine, rain, or warm, still, scented dark, on the lake life seems very good. Once again I should give thanks that my lot has fallen in such pleasant country ways.

*   *   *   *   *   *

This evening Charlie, my pupil, and I went for a drive in order to watch Wiltshire's farming genius busy with the tail end of his haymaking. Of course, the farm buildings were practically deserted when we arrived, but a blacksmith, black, brawny, sweaty, and busy over his fire, grunted some directions. " Down thic 'ill, turn left-'anded droo a gate opposite a thatched cottage, an' you cain't miss it. I 'low you kin drive till you do find 'em, fer there's a sight o' cars there a'ready. The guvner's away, but I 'low 'ee'll be back any minnit, jist to buck things up a bit."

Through that gate we went, nursed the car carefully along a tyre-worn track across a pasture, safely negotiated two wooden cow-bridges, and arrived at a hayfield where the crop was being harvested. I parked the car under the hedge near three or four practically new motor-bikes, and then we walked over to a rick which was about half finished.

A small oil-engine stuttered as it drove the elevator. Two motor-cars, one an English saloon of ancient vintage, and the other the remains of what had been a high-powered American two-seater, were busy pushing haysweeps in front of them. In turn they pushed their loads to the foot of the elevator, then reversed, leaving their loads behind, and in the space of a few minutes, moments almost, they were back with another load. Three men were on the rick and two were on the ground forking a constant stream of hay into the elevator.

There was nothing new to any of us in this outfit. It was just a nicely-balanced small gang of men and machines. But each man knew his job, and was performing it with the minimum of effort. Of course, the front wheels of the elevator had been discarded in order to lower the feeding point by about two feet. Two feet saved, when you are lifting hay on a fork from eight a.m. until eight p.m., is a dickens of a lot.

To get the same amount of hay ricked by old-time methods would have entailed as follows: six wagons, six horses at least and most likely eight, for two trace horses would have been used for the loaded wagons, four men pitching in the field, four men loading on the wagons, four boys leading, four men unloading the wagons, and about six men on the rick. To give this team their due they would have put up a slightly tidier rick; but against this they would have left behind them three times the amount of raking, for the modern haysweep picks up hay in much cleaner fashion than the hand pitcher.

In the next field we found a similar outfit, and from one of its members I gathered the information that over the hedge there was a stacker at work instead of an elevator. We arrived there just as the men were finishing pegging down this latest monstrosity, and so were able to see a rick start from zero.

A young man in a tangerine and black jazz shirt with beret to match threw down a huge hammer which he had been using to drive in a peg, yelled "Oke," clambered into a car, and backed swiftly away from the site of the proposed rick. Two other cars did likewise. A brawny individual leaned over the wheel of yet another car in blissful, bored content.

Thirty seconds later things began to happen. Master tangerine shirt arrived *en* automobile, pushing a sweep-load of hay. He pushed it on to another sweep at the front of the stacker, and backed swiftly away. The brawny chauffeur in the other car then woke to life. His car was attached to the stacker by a wire cable, and as it backed swiftly away, the stacker rose upwards like a miniature flip-flap, and literally flopped the sweep-load of hay on to the rick site. As it returned to the rank, so to speak, the stacker descended to receive another load from the next car. Then back went the stacker's car, and up went the load as before.

In half an hour as I watched that rick grew like a mushroom, and the crop in the field seemed to melt away. There were, I think, five or six men on the rick, and as each load tumbled down they swarmed over it like beavers. Apparently everyone was a rickmaker, and this was necessary for they had to deal with a steady average of two sweep-loads of hay per minute.

We were so interested in watching the business and in seeing that we were not run over—there are no pedestrian crossings in a Wiltshire hayfield; anyone there who is fool enough to walk on his two flat feet must look out for himself—that I did not see the " Guvner " arrive until his car was almost on top of me. " Glad to see you," he shouted when I turned. " Excuse me a minute or two. Shan't be long, but this job needs balancing." And away over the field he went.

I could not see much wrong with the existing arrangements, but in ten minutes I could see the effect of a master hand. One car and sweep was taken away from the field where the rick was being finished and added to the stacker outfit. Result, the occasional thirty-second pause in the stacker's movements was obliterated. The other elevator gang were admonished to lay their rick out a trifle so that the whole crop of that field could be put into it. Then back came the " Guvner " to the stacker. He took one look at the rick and another at the field, and then gave orders for this rick to be contracted in size. Then he lit a cigarette and deigned to talk to me. " Good fellows," he said, referring to his employees, " but they won't look ahead. If I hadn't nipped back here this rick would have been only half a rick, and there'd a bin some three or four ton o' hay over in t'other field. Still, we've put up a hundred ton a day this week."

We stood together and watched his haymaking orchestra responding to the control of a first-class conductor. The stacker field was a small one of about fifteen acres, and the crop was a good ton per acre. Carrying started at six p.m., and it was evident that before eight o'clock the field would be cleared. The men engaged were of all types—young university men, casual town workmen from the labour exchange, and Wessex farm labourers of all ages. Clean-shaven, unshaven, or grey-bearded, all were agricultural engineers willy-nilly, for the horse was conspicuous by its absence. The best comment on the whole business came from my pupil. " Those folks who think that any fool can farm successfully should visit that outfit," he remarked.

On the way home we noticed that harvest had begun, for we passed several fields of winter oats already up in stook.

* * * * * *

From my establishment's point of view there is only one way of describing to-day, and that is to call it " A great day." For to-day our jockey made her debut at a village gymkhana. Consequently her day began early. Immediately after breakfast she groomed Toby until he shone. At eleven o'clock a neighbouring amateur rider and friend of the family—our one and only Cherub, four feet nothing of country craft, horsemanship, and rural courtesy—arrived on his pony to lead Toby to the scene of operations. Thereafter our entrant worried that she might arrive late, and that Toby might never arrive. She ate almost nothing for lunch, and fairly drove the household into the car in good time.

We arrived a good hour before the start, and while we were waiting Cherub gave us the low-down—there is no other word which so well describes his remarks—on the coming contest and the other competitors. Several years of Cherub's friendship have taught me to respect his judgment, especially in financial matters, and I will back that boy to make his running expenses in any walk of life. He is one of the few remaining individualists amongst modern youth. As I knew that his customary practice was to make gymkhanas pay, I was even more ready to take his advice.

Open jumping, jumping under seventeen, and the handy hunter were, he told me, beyond his capabilities, which definitely ruled them out for Pam. I was a trifle surprised at his decision to miss the handy hunter, for in walking round the course I could not see anything much to trouble him, and I said as much.

"Waste of money, Mr. Street," he replied. "You see, there's Peggy This and Mr. That, and young Tom So-and-so. I haven't a ghost of a chance against them, and there's only three prizes, so what's the use of wasting two shillings to enter?"

Out of the mouths of lads like Cherub comes sound counsel in these matters, so I told Pam that she must be content with things like potato races and musical chairs, and her mother that sufficient for the day should be the risks thereof.

Alas for Pam's pride and hopes! All the other competitors were polished performers, and she was sadly behind them. Still, she did win her first heat in the potato race, the reason being that the other three riders—amongst them Cherub—either let their mounts kick over the buckets or dropped a potato on the ground. So Pam, slow and sure and very intent, won that heat, to her great surprise, and to her great joy that she had beaten Cherub. But in the final she was outclassed.

Cherub won the musical chairs, first prize fifteen shillings, and left the ring in triumph. Later he came second in the bending race, another five shillings safely netted, and then he was prepared to call it a day. There was but one other race, a wheelbarrow race. "No good to me," he explained. "I'm not strong enough to push a barrow against these others, and I can't very well let a girl push me." I do hope I live to see Cherub grow

Potatoe Race

up, and so perhaps be able to admire his procedure when girls become more important to him. I should imagine that he will carefully select some damsel, and then cut her out from the herd in approved cowpuncher style. Of one thing I'm certain. That girl will not know anything about it until he has her safely hogtied.

But Pam had no such qualms about being pushed, and with the help of another girl she came second in this race, and in due course received a blue rosette and a half-crown. Then came the crowning joy of the day. I persuaded her mother to allow her to ride home with Cherub, a full twelve miles. As we were waiting to see them set off I saw a pretty sight: a groom coming across the sun-drenched pasture on a sixteen-hand hunter, leading four little ponies, two on either side. Why is it that all grooms and hunt servants look so much alike? The same chiselled features, the same thin lips, and the same poker face. This man had done very well this afternoon in the open jumping; afterwards he had coached and encouraged his youthful charges in their events; and now he was going home with their mounts and his own. If they held gymkhanas a hundred years ago it would have been a very similar figure who took the mounts home afterwards, for the English groom is a national institution.

We heard our cross-country riders coming up the road to the farm about nine o'clock, and of course went out to meet them. Cherub had a red and a blue rosette in his bridle, and Pam one blue one in hers; and, incredible as it may seem, on each of their small faces shone a grin fully a foot wide. Somehow I think that a pony gymkhana is better than the cinema as a treat for young children.

They were both obviously dog-tired, so I offered to put Cherub's pony up, and to drive him home the remaining three miles. He thanked me courteously, but said that he had better ride home. Then he swept off his cap and clattered away. That child consumes his own smoke.

* * * * * *

There seems to be no end to the uses of the motor-car in farming, and more and more the garage proprietor is becoming an agricultural engineer. One of my neighbours in that line of business has just put upon the market a most curious machine. He has married an old motor-car to a five-feet grass-mower, and the result of this unholy alliance appears to be a most useful tool. I am no engineer, but this is apparently the method of construction. The body of the car is removed, and instead of the back wheels a cog is fitted on either end of the back axle. The mower is placed so that these cogs mesh in the driving wheels, the cardan shaft of the car being shortened to bring the mower close enough to the steering wheel of the car. A spring seat is fitted, giving easy control of both car and mower; and the result is a light tractor which can be used for mowing, or, with the cutter bar removed, for pushing a sweep, hauling a side-rake, and possibly, under certain conditions, for some light two-furrow ploughing. I am going to make it my business to see this machine in actual work over a long day, for, on the face of it, it appears to be just the cheap light tractor for which the small, mainly grass, farmer has been looking for some time.

But now haymaking is behind us for this season and harvest is here. I walked up to my wheat this evening, and discovered that the last few days of sunshine had ripened it tremendously. In fact, it is all but, and the next few days shall see it in stook.

August

Harvest is in full swing. Where wheat crops are good this year they are very good, and in some places they have been badly laid by thunderstorms. On one farm to-day I saw a field in which various methods of reaping were in evidence. There were a tractor binder, a horse binder, a grass mower, and three men with scythes, all busy.

Whenever and wherever you see this sort of thing you will find almost invariably that the scythe men are between sixty and seventy years old, for to-day youth controls the machine and age does the hand work. Still, our climate will always make it necessary for a few men on each farm to learn to mow, and no youthful tractor driver should consider it beneath his dignity to swing a scythe on occasion. It's a satisfactory job, too, with a nice feel to it, and the song of the scythe takes some beating. That sight of hand-mowing to-day recalled a line of white-shirted backs in the water-meadows some twenty years ago, and I almost fancied I could hear the music they made—swish—swish—swish.

And that reminds me of a remark made by an Irish labourer whom one of my neighbours had engaged for the haymaking. Rain having stopped the carrying, my friend asked him if he could use a scythe to trim out a pikked corner of a field, with which the tractor mower could not deal satisfactorily. " Send one along and I'll try," he replied. An hour later my friend drove up the road and shouted over the hedge, asking how the scythe was going. " Goes right well," came the reply. " I got a divil of a job to keep up wi' un."

* * * * * *

My own wheat was cut to-day. As my corn-growing is too small to warrant the possession of a binder, I had arranged with a neighbour to come with a tractor binder and cut my one field of seventeen acres. Rummy how one's farming changes. Seven years ago I grew three hundred acres of corn per annum, and possessed two eight-feet-cut tractor binders. Now I grow but one small field and have to hire someone to do my cutting.

As usual, we began cutting in a fashion which earned the outspoken disapproval of Jim, the drowner. It was a good upstanding piece of wheat, and I gave orders for the tractor and binder to drive straight round it without having first mown and cleared a path for the engine. "I'd be ashamed fer to do sich wickedness," said old Jim, when he found out what was going to happen. "I tell 'ee, 'tis hrong."

To one who has a tidy eye and no thought of making farming pay, cutting round a piece of corn with the scythe and hand-tying the swath is a very nice thing to do, but from a fairly extensive experience of harvesting corn both in this country and in Canada, I know that it does not pay. More than that, I am sure that it wastes much more corn than to drive straight through the standing crop with either horses or tractor, and later on to cut back the reverse way. If the latter operation is done carefully very little corn will be missed, whereas the scythe and subsequent hand-tying leaves a lot scattered about on the ground.

It is difficult to write dialect just as it is spoken, but the Wiltshire version of certain words which begin with an R necessitates the prefixing of an H in order to obtain a little of the local flavour in the written form. So, 'hright' or 'hrong' we drove through the crop this morning in the face of Jim's sour disapproval.

But if I did wrong early to-day, I had occasion later to point out to Jim that he was not doing as rightly as he should. This was in the quality of his stooking. I have always noticed that the Wiltshire farm labourer makes a poor fist at this job. True, he plods on and stooks a fair acreage per day, but he *leans* the sheaves against each other, which makes a poor stook which will not stand up to the slightest puff of wind. The right way and the only way to stook is to drive the butt of each sheaf firmly into the ground.

I feel that I can speak with some authority in this matter of stooking, for I stooked two hundred acres of grain single-handed for four consecutive harvests in Western Canada. When a man has to keep up with an eight-foot binder and cook his own grub, and also stick up on Sundays any stooks which have fallen down, he puts them up firmly the first time. I am badly out of condition now, but ten years ago I could stook twice as quickly and ten times as well as any workman in this district, a fact which I have demonstrated to the men on this farm. Like the immortal Lem Putt in Mr. Charles Sale's classic book, *The Specialist*, I have studied the art of stooking and specialised in performing it better than the average. If he were to write my ideas of the best type of stook, it would go something like this:

"When it comes to construction I can give you round stooks or long stooks. Long ones are a little more trouble to make, but they're worth it, and I'll tell you why. Both sorts stand well, but for quick drying give me the long stook of ten sheaves. I've studied both sorts in all weathers. To make the long stook properly erect a double row of three sheaves, and then two sheaves on either side placed to lock where the sheaves on the inner rows touch each other. And be sure to handle each sheaf like you would a crowbar. Then you'll have no need to go round every morning and put up the fallen stooks, 'cause there won't be any, an' you'll have a mighty pretty corn field till you rick 'em."

Imitation is the sincerest form of flattery, but in this case how obviously is it imitation!

* * * * * *

What a firm hold the glory of the corn harvest has in all our minds, no matter whether we be townsfolk or countryfolk! Corn-growing in this island to-day is a very minor branch of our farming industry, and its success or failure makes little or no difference to the lives of our huge town population. Yet you very rarely, practically never, hear a townsman ask his farmer friends how the cows are milking or how the hens are laying, but you often hear him asking about the well-being of the corn harvest. And the farmer, even such an inveterate grass-farmer as I, even if his corn harvest is an infinitesimal proportion of his business, obtains more joy and satisfaction from it than from the larger and more prosaic though more profitable branches of his farming.

The reason is the remembrance of the Bible stories which most of us learned at our mothers' knees, and, of course, because the corn harvest is the most spectacular and possibly the most beautiful scene of the farming year. People can see and admire a cornfield both before and after it is cut, even when driving swiftly along a road; but a herd of cows, a flock of sheep, poultry houses, and pigs, all much bigger things in a financial sense, do not fill the eye of the beholder, although perhaps the last does fill his nose.

Anyway, I know that I obtain more joy each year from my little bit of wheat than from either my cows or my haymaking. Logically this is absurd, but actually it is a fact which defies all argument. Some two years ago I had no corn harvest of any kind, and during a fine August I felt like a man who was out of work, or a deserter from the army. Somehow I could not be happy on my own farm, and went poking about the country-side looking at other people's harvesting, and wishing that I could join in the fun ; for I refuse to call corn-harvesting a fray, although that word fittingly describes haymaking.

* * * * * *

With the wheat in aisle, but not yet fit to stack, to-day seemed to be a good chance to go fishing on the Wylye, a day's holiday which takes some beating. Glorious sunshine all day, a good rise of black gnat about 11.30, and thereafter precious little doing until seven o'clock, when the river was popping all over for about half an hour. But how much more wily is the trout than the grayling ! Yet, in spite of this, the river teems with grayling, and anglers are besought to kill these fish irrespective of size.

Apparently they spoil the trout fishing by rushing in to take the fly which has been cast carefully for a rising trout, and so putting him down immediately. Consequently, expert fishermen would like to see the river cleared of them ; but moderate performers such as I appreciate their presence, for it enables us always to take home something. However, to-day I managed to snaffle two takeable trout, one just over and one just under two pounds, in addition to six brace of good grayling.

The second trout, the smaller one, was pure luck, for I never saw him until he came over the net. I cast into the mill pool during the evening rise, he wanted my fly, rushed for it, and that was that after five minutes' battle. But the first fish was a work of art. He was lying underneath the arch of a stone bridge, and from downstream I watched him rise several times. What little breeze was against me, and a blackberry bush trailed into the water a foot or two below him, making things still more awkward. Anyone who has fished the Wylye around that lovely village of Wishford will recognise the spot.

He was at least two feet under the arch, and lay close against the wall of the bridge. Somehow or other my fly must be cast to shoot under the bridge, hit the wall just above the fish, and thence drop like gossamer just in front of his eager mouth. For three-quarters of an hour I laboured while he rose at other flies with maddening regularity. I lost three flies in the blackberry bush, and the breeze saw to it that my best casts dropped a full foot short of the fish. And over me and all the meadows shone an August sun.

An old-age pensioner of my acquaintance toddled by during this contest, and perched himself on a fallen elm butt to watch the fun. "Artful card, 'ee be," he remarked oracularly. "I've a zeed a main vew gennelmen tryin' fer 'im thease summer. 'Mazin' 'ow they knows jist where to git, bain't it?"

I agreed, and during an interval in my labours while I was putting on a new fly I gave him my pouch. "Thank 'ee kindly," he said, and added, "I 'low thic veller's gwaine to do 'ee." "Shouldn't wonder," I replied, "but we'll give him another quarter of an hour."

And towards the end of that fifteen minutes came triumph. A black gnat hit the wall, stuck there for a moment, and then dropped just in the right place. A natural fly, obviously, for no angler could cast in that spot, or so thought the fish. He took it gently, and was greatly astonished and annoyed to find himself in trouble. Down stream into the pool below the bridge he rushed, and there for ten good minutes he led me a pretty dance. As soon as he was safely out on the bank I looked at my ancient spectator. "Something attempted, Granfer, something done. It's supposed to earn a night's repose, but just now I reckon lunch would go down well. What about you drinking his health?" Here I pointed to the fish. "Wall! 'Tis nigh on one, zur, an' I 'low as I could toddle as fur as the Swan." So to the Swan we toddled, and there we toasted my triumph in much good brown ale, whilst we watched an exciting dart match between some local experts.

Somehow a day on the Wylye is the best way of spending a summer day that I know. Even if the fishing luck be poor the day is always a pleasant one. The Wylye is a very narrow valley, in places not more than a half-mile from main road to by-road, and in consequence one always feels cosy and comfortable in its meadows. The hills on either side rise very sharply from the meadow land, and to-day the standing corn and corn in aisle made a charming picture as I saw it from the river bank.

To me the great charm of the water-meadows is that they have been able to defy nearly all the modern machinery which has effected such changes in the farming of most of our countryside. Here the tractor cannot come; neither can the portable milking machine, nor the implements of cultivation. Hence the water-meadows remain unchanged, a green haven of peace and beauty for the idler, the haunt of those who appreciate the difficulties and joy of that artistic sport, dry-fly fishing; and the one remaining home of hand-work in the land.

But let no one think that dry-fly fishing is an easy job on a hot day. There was not a dry stitch on me when I got home this evening, and soon afterwards the inner man was moistened to match. And now bed, for there's trout for breakfast in the morning.

* * * * * *

I called on a neighbour to-day about some business, and found him up in the harvest field where he was carrying some winter oats, a nice crop. Here again was a horseless field, for the sheaves were being conveyed to the foot of the elevator by

The Water meadows remain unchanged

motor-car sweeps, and, as usual, the elevator was being driven by a small oil engine instead of by the horse gear of my youth.

And again the same effect of most recent farming changes was to be seen—a cheaper method of doing the job, but a resultant destruction of charm. It seemed wrong somehow to see a crop of corn being ricked without a sight of a wagon piled high with sheaves trundling slowly towards the rick, and I said as much to my friend. "We've destroyed all the romance and beauty in our calling," I remarked, "and we don't make half the money our fathers did." "True," he said, "but neither your father nor mine would be able to keep their farms, much less make a decent living out of them, if they carried on to-day with the old-time methods. And let me tell you that both of them would be doing just the same as we do if they were alive to-day, for they were hustlers during harvest as you and I well know."

I grinned in remembrance, for my own father had seemed a heavy cross for me to bear when I first left school, and I knew that his had been cast in similar mould. "Yes," I said, "my old man would have thoroughly approved of the work those sweeps are doing."

"So would mine. Gosh, but he was a slave-driver when the sun was shining. Do you know what he said to me once in front of the men when I was sixteen?"

"No! Tell me," I chuckled.

"Well, I had been at the rick all day from six in the morning, and it was a hot, thundery day. I was about whacked by six o'clock. You know how hot it can be when a rick's in the sun and out of the breeze?"

"Rather!" I nodded.

"Father rode up on his horse just as it was my turn to empty a load of wheat sheaves up into the pitch-hole. He sat there and timed me, and when I finished he shut his watch with a snap, and said, ' Jack ! you'll die in the workhouse.' "

On my way home I thought about this, and remembered a remark made to me by a dairyman when I had left school about three months. Somehow or other I had crossed him, and received a lecture for my sins, which finished up with : "And every night when you goes to bed thee't best pray that thee father'll live vive minnits longer than thee, fer thee uttent keep theeself vive minnits atter 'ee's gone." There doesn't seem to be much doubt of his opinion of me, does there ? The true countryman is rarely ambiguous in his remarks.

But the curious thing is that I never bore any animosity against that man. When my father died he became my right-hand man, the highest paid man on my farm, and the one to whom I always turned for advice and wise counsel in any difficulty. And glad am I that when I sold my retail milk business I was able to make it possible for him to buy and to run it, a thing which he is still doing in admirable fashion. These efficient countryfolk may have been hard in their treatment of youth, but that treatment leaves no nasty taste in my mouth, but rather an increasing admiration as the years pass. And I know that my friend of this afternoon would say the same. Of course, perhaps this tolerance of ours is because we have proved our critics wrong, in that my friend has not yet come to the workhouse, and I have managed to keep myself since my father's death. But I don't think that is the only reason or the major one ; which is that while they might have been harsh with us they were always just, and so earned our respect rather than our hatred.

* * * * * *

To-day and yesterday we have been carrying wheat, and to-night about seven o'clock saw everything safely ricked, so another corn harvest in my life has come and gone. Needless to say we swept the crop in with the car sweep. This does not look a pretty job—in fact, at first sight it looks all wrong—but I took particular notice to-day to find out whether it wasted much corn. I drove the sweep myself while the milkers were away for the afternoon milking, and when they returned I rode in to the rick once or twice on the dumb-irons of the car in order to see if much corn was rubbed out in transit. Provided the sweep is not overloaded so that some sheaves are pushed in front of it along the stubble I am convinced that this method of harvesting sheds far less corn than the pitcher and loader and wagon. Which, of course, is one up again for modernity, for in cost and in speed the sweep wins easily.

The lad who works on the open-air milking outfit asked me after tea whether he could get off at six as he had a ticket for the Tidworth Tattoo; and as the job was obviously going to be finished before knock-off time at eight o'clock without his help, I told him to push off immediately. He will get back to-morrow morning, just about in time to start milking. Now, in my middle-age, to do that sort of thing seems hardly worth while, but I did it at his age. Anyway, I would sooner have one lad of that temperament than half a dozen of the born-tired breed. The old dairyman's comment on this business puts it admirably. "You kin do anythin' wi' a colt, ef zo be as 'ee'll goo. 'Tis when they wun't goo no road at all that they be wuss than useless."

* * * * * *

Jim began thatching the wheat ricks to-day, and this morning I drove up to find out how many more bundles of thatch he would require. Coming home I could not help noticing what a shaven look the countryside had. Haymaking was late and many fields still showed barren in brown and green streaks.

Most of the corn, in fact all save the late barley, was cut, and a large proportion of it carried; and as root crops are few and far between in this district nowadays, the trees in the landscape showed up very distinctly, like green pimples on a shaven cheek.

Once harvest is over a farmer begins to think of sport, and last night, just as we were finishing wheat-carting, I noticed some wild duck passing over on their evening flight. I never enjoy shooting wild duck down in the meadows in early August. They don't expect to be shot at, and in the majority of cases when you flush them they present such easy targets. But wild duck when they are flighting in the twilight or perhaps the moonlight are well worth while. So, after supper this evening, my wife and I drove up to the top of the downs to see if we could bag a dinner.

My father always enjoyed doing this, and I remembered that when he changed his hammer-gun for a hammerless he found that he could not hit duck in the late August and September evenings anything like so well with the new weapon. After one evening's comparative failure he decided that with the old hammer-gun, if he got a glimpse of a duck between the horns of the hammers, down it came. So he obtained a piece of stiffish leather, pressed the barrels of his gun down on it to make a mark, and then cut along the mark so that the leather would slip down along the barrels. Then he cut this into two horns, thus making a rude but effective backsight for his new gun. I rummaged about in the storeroom where I keep all sorts of relics until I found this aid to efficiency, and I must say that it is a good tip for anyone to copy.

This evening I had five shots and bagged two brace of duck, a most satisfactory performance, for they did not come over in very easy fashion. As a great treat we took my old retriever, Trinket, with us in the car. She is a faithful old golden friend, but now too stiff to walk far, and too deaf to behave properly in company, but her nose is as good as ever. Leave her to take her own time after a wounded bird or animal, and she'll trot up with it sooner or later, wriggling and grinning in ecstasy. One duck went down in a long stagger a full hundred yards behind me into the middle of a large patch of gorse and thorn and brambles. Away into the gloom trotted Trinket, whilst I, knowing that I could be of no help to her in that light, lit a cigarette and waited.

No more duck came over, so twenty minutes afterwards we decided to call it a day, and walked back towards the scrub to call Trinket to give up the hunt. By then it was almost pitch dark, and we could neither see nor hear anything moving in the cover. I whistled and called without much hope, for I knew that Trinket would not hear me if she were twenty yards away. Nothing happened for another ten minutes, and so we decided to wait in the car until Trinket should condescend to come home with us. But as we walked towards it a wolfish shadow met us with the missing duck in its mouth.

* * * * * *

This afternoon I drove some eight miles in order to watch a combine harvester at work on a neighbour's farm, and this evening while I was dipping into Richard Jefferies' *Wild Life in a Southern County* I came across this passage:

> "In the autumn after the harvest the gleaning is still an important time to the cottager, though nothing like it used to be. Reaping by machinery has made rapid inroads, and there is not nearly so much left behind as in former days. Yet half the women and children of the place go out and glean, but very few now bake at home; they have their bread from the baker, who comes round in the smallest hamlets. Possibly they had a more wholesome article in the

olden time, when the wheat from their gleanings was ground at the village mill, and the flour made into bread at home. But the coming of the mechanician has invaded the ancient customs: the very sheaves are now to be bound with wire by the same machine that reaps the corn. The next generation of country folk will hardly be able to understand the story of Ruth."

Somehow I feel like writing a similar paragraph, for the combine harvester has robbed the harvest field of as much charm for me as the self-binder did for Jefferies. He mourned the passing of the gleaners, and I feel tempted to mourn the passing of the sheaf and the stook. It is the same old story—each new method, while it may increase the efficiency of farming, robs my calling of some of its romance and charm.

In this instance I am not convinced that farming gains very much, if anything, in efficiency. In a few isolated cases of large farms of suitable land this new method of harvesting may be more economic than the binder, but for the average farm I cannot budget it to show a profit. The combine will cut corn and thrash it cleanly enough in dry weather—of that there is no doubt—but the wakes of short straw and cavings and chaff which it leaves behind cause me furiously to think. If they are burnt immediately the straw will be wasted. If wet weather comes they cannot be either burnt or collected; and even in dry weather they cannot be burnt on new seeds. In either case it would seem that the straw, instead of being an asset, becomes a liability. And then there is the cost of drying the newly-threshed grain to be considered.

But I expect I am like Jefferies. I am hunting for faults and refusing to recognise virtues, simply because I mourn the loss of charm. New men, new methods, and as the farmer cannot live on charm there is no doubt that the combine has come to stay in certain parts of this island. Its increasing use illustrates once again that the British farmer is a trier, and a man who will use every new invention to help him in his fight to compete with the overseas producer. Who am I to criticise his methods? I swept my wheat with a motor-car, and there was precious little beauty in that operation. Indeed, I think that the combine is superior to the sweep in this respect. As one watches it from a distance it seems like a great ship passing slowly and in stately fashion round and round the huge square of standing grain. It is only when one gets close to it that its true character, that of a snorting, hideous, all-consuming Moloch, is apparent.

On my way home I passed a harvest field of the old type: wagons and horses and trace horses and boys and men and stooks and a chunky rick with the westering sun throwing its squat shadow on the stubble. The modern farmer part of me said, "H'm! That's an expensive hobby," while the sentimentalist in me pulled up his car in order to savour the charm of his boyhood's harvest once again.

* * * * * *

Modern transport facilities have made possible to the villager so many new interests that village cricket has lost much of its one-time popularity. In fact, each year sees an increasing number of villages without a team, and local cricket survives only where there is a district league, or in the village which possesses a cricketing enthusiast who is both able and willing to take the running of a team to play friendlies entirely on his own shoulders. Of the two types I prefer the latter, for the former often brings into the game the worst side of organised competition, bad feeling amongst the players.

The other day I was privileged to spend a gloriously lazy, pleasant, and interesting afternoon watching a friendly match between two village teams. There was no doubt that

Village Cricket

much of the pleasure of both players and spectators was derived from the setting of the scene. On one side of the ground ran a placid chalk trout stream with here and there a willow or a poplar along its banks. On the opposite boundary were tall elm trees, through which one obtained glimpses of cosy thatched cottages, a half-timbered farmhouse, and the grey stone tower of a church. And over all shone an August sun, a sun which had finished an early harvest, and thus set free the farming members of the team, who usually have to say good-bye to cricket from July until mid-September.

Rural wages being higher in comparison with food prices than they have ever been in my memory, every player boasted white flannel trousers, but here and there a bright-coloured shirt surmounted them, and in one case the pleasing effect of immaculate trousers and white shirt on fifteen stone of Wiltshire brawn was enhanced by bright green braces. These were worn by "Our Ernie," who works for the wheelwright. He is blessed with bright, unruly red hair and a cheerful, adventurous disposition, both, to my mind, great assets to his side; for the one adds to the gaiety of the scene, and the other to the gaiety of the cricket. They would be badly off without "Our Ernie."

I sat beneath the shade of an elm and talked with the vicar while the visitors batted. In his youth he was a fine cricketer; and I think that even now at sixty-nine he is too much of a purist to appreciate "Our Ernie's" vicious hooks to square leg at their proper worth. But to him cricket of any kind is better than no cricket at all, and as long as he lives there will be cricket in his village.

The match was timed to start at three, and at twenty-five minutes past that hour it started. By tea-time, half-past four, the visitors had made fifty-seven, and by the time they were all out for one hundred and twenty-five there was only an hour's play remaining. Obviously it was impossible for the home side to win in the time, so in approved style the opening bats proceeded to poke in order to save the game. There were two reasons for this procedure. One was the legacy of some two seasons ago when the team had played league cricket, in which an inglorious draw was reckoned to be better than a glorious defeat; and the other was the effect of modern communication which has enabled rural cricketers to read and hear detailed information concerning the latest cricketing methods.

Accordingly, they poked for half an hour for fifteen runs in such tedious fashion that there was an audible murmur of relief when the local builder's foreman edged an easy catch into first slip's hands. Immediately there was a cry amongst the spectators for "Our Ernie." "Let 'Our Ernie' 'ave a goo, maister," said Granfer Yates to the skipper, a young farmer and his one-time employer. This worthy grinned and yielded to popular clamour, whereupon "Our Ernie" marched forth to battle. Batting gloves he scorned, and his one pad flapped as he walked towards the wicket, while his hair stood up like the hogged red mane of a pony, which had escaped the clippers for at least two months. "Noo we shall zee zummat," said Granfer. And "zee zummat" we did.

In the language of the cricketing journalist "Our Ernie" proceeded to "have a go," a thing which he did with marked success. The first ball he hit into the road for four. Off the second he ran one, and "over" was called. While the players were running across we could hear him saying to the umpire with regard to his last stroke, "I didn' rightly ketch 'ee." In the next over he proceeded to "ketch" them very rightly.

The fielding side had evidently experienced a taste of his quality before, for they had massed themselves on the leg side near the river. But they need not have bothered. "Our Ernie" recked naught of fielders, and smote the ball into the river every time. By the time five balls had been bowled he had four in the river, and as there were no more available the game had to be held up for a few minutes while the results of his prowess were fished out. He made a glorious forty-seven before he was bowled neck and crop by that deadly village cricket ball, a shooter.

Naturally, we gave him an ovation on his return to the elms, and even the vicar was moved to murmur to me, "Not quite according to Cocker, but great fun while it lasted." Which, to my mind, was less than its due, for as a result the home side drew the match with eighty-odd for five wickets when stumps were drawn. I prefer to call Ernie's performance great fun and great cricket under the circumstances, and I argued as much with the vicar as I drove him back to the vicarage, where he continued to differ in courteous fashion over a glass of fine sherry. But in one thing we were at one, and that was that modern village life is the better for a little friendly cricket mixed with the town amusements which modern invention has brought to the village dweller; or, as my host put it, that the future village should obtain the best of both worlds, the charm of the old and the amenities of the new.

September

"And one man in his time plays many parts"– so said Shakespeare; and no one, I imagine, disagrees with that statement. But I have a notion that a farmer plays a greater number than most folk. There is no certainty about his life. In actual fact he lives from day to day in what may best be described as an atmosphere of battle, murder, and sudden death, with here and there some births in due season. Even this grass farming of mine has its moments. I never know what time I shall be going to bed, nor when I may be called to get up. Night, I grant, holds a farm in leash, so to speak, but it is always straining to get away: waiting eagerly for dawn to give permission.

In the space of one twenty-four hours I may be a farmer, a chauffeur, a mechanic, a navvy, a midwife, a sportsman, a groom, a carter, a cowman, a gardener, a buyer, a seller, a financier—I include that because it was pay-day to-day—and almost countless other things. In addition, I have the cares and pleasures of being a peddler of words, which makes life indeed a busy business. But how much better is this varied career than that settled groove from house to office!

This morning I visited a bunch of in-calf heifers, and arrived just in time to help Charlie with a calving case. It was more than a one-man job, but together we managed to bring it to a successful conclusion. Somehow I find it very satisfying to do this sort of thing: to feel that for once I have done something worth while, and thereby justified my existence. Writing about farming is all very well, but it cannot be compared with doing it. When I am busy at some urgent job on the farm what may or may not be happening in the great world outside my little bit of Wiltshire fades away into insignificance. This morning Charlie and I have saved the life of a calf. There are a good many folk who have done less. Which is a splendidly self-satisfied thought with which to go to bed.

* * * * * *

Somehow or other until to-day I had not been to one agricultural show this summer. The larger ones had clashed with other appointments, and the largest, the Royal, which I always try to attend, came bang in the middle of a late hay-making. Nowadays I am often guilty of running away from my farm to other interests, but as long as I have a farm I shall be on parade for haymaking. That business just won't go without the master's eye, or so I and most farmers think. So to-day I endeavoured to make amends for my sins of omission, and attended a local show.

One show is very like another. No matter what difference there may be in importance, each one illustrates the complexity and size of our farming industry, which to-day seems to do business with almost every industry in the country. At least, so it seemed to me this morning as I walked along the rows of trade stands.

I do not think many farmers ever attend a show without buying something, or at any rate making up their minds to buy something when the season to use it comes round. To-day, as I was driving to the show ground I decided that I did not want anything, having at last got my farm tricked out to run as a dairy farm, which, while it does not pay much, does pay a little even in these difficult days. But now that all farming is largely performed by mechanical means what farmer can resist a new gadget.? Certainly not I, and the attractions of a handy adjustable spanner and a wire strainer proved too much for me.

But if I did not buy very much I carefully examined every new implement shown, and wrangled with my friends concerning their advantages and disadvantages. And that, I think, is one of the most important features of a show: it does provide facilities for farmers to argue about farming methods, and in this way to gain much useful information from each other. Anyway, my friends and I wrangled amicably about machinery and livestock and all sorts of things until and during lunch.

Which reminds me of a show lunch with a friend some three years ago. It was an important show, and boasted an enormous luncheon tent. For sweet we ordered fruit salad, and when it arrived the waiter asked us whether we would like some custard with it, whereupon my friend asked for cream. The waiter said that there was none to be had, and then the storm broke.

"This is an agricultural show," said my companion. "If we can't get cream for lunch here, how in the devil can we expect restaurants and hotels to supply it?"

"I'm sorry, sir," said the waiter, "but it's not my fault that there's only custard."

"True, brother, true," came the reply, "but it's somebody's fault. Custard! We give that stuff to pigs. And dammit, think of all the papers yappin' about over-production of milk! By God! I'll have some cream or wreck the place. There's some dairy cows here, ain't there? And a butter-makin' contest? Where's the man in charge?"

By this time the whole company was interested in the argument, for he did not whisper his plaint. The catering manager came, and in a few minutes we had fresh thick cream for everybody present. I have often thought about that little episode. Most of us will put up with anything rather than raise our voices or cause a scene. Which, while it may be good manners, is not a virtue which obtains redress for real grievances. The man who will dare to be awkward in public in a just cause commands my respect, for I recognise that he is a better man than I am. Since my friend demanded cream for his lunch at that show I have always found it on the menu, and there it was to-day.

After lunch I spent an hour watching the horses in the big ring. Hackneys were a good class, which rather surprised me, for I cannot see that the harness trotter fulfils a useful purpose to any great extent in the nation's life to-day, and feel certain that in the near future this type of horse will become less important. But there is no doubt he does look fine as he bangs along in front of his owner, who is seated in a vehicle which looks more like a cross between a bicycle and a pram than anything else.

Show jumping, in spite of the increasing use of the motor-car by all classes of people, seems to get better and better. This afternoon there were more clear rounds than faulted ones, and once again the ladies were very much to the fore. It is a fascinating business to watch, but somehow I cannot think that the horses get much fun out of it. They never get a chance to have a real go at any obstacle. Per-ump, per-ump, per-ump, and then let him go, and he's over, seems to be the prevailing fashion. I can, or perhaps it would be safer to say I could, sit a horse taking a jump in his stride; but I have no desire to attempt this slow, cat-footed approach, and then the almost direct up and down which follows.

I was sorry that I could not stay to see the children jumping, but as I had a bunch of in-calf heifers arriving from Ireland at six o'clock, I had to get home in time to help get them down from the station. Funny how a farmer's life is ruled by his animals! Some folks say that man was made for something better than to toil for his living by waiting on the needs of farm livestock; but I fancy that many other ways of getting a living are less noble, and certainly less satisfying to the getter. Work we must, in spite of modern inventions, and it is well to be able to love one's work, a thing which most countrymen seem to do. Why? Simply because without that love farming rarely succeeds.

Very certainly everybody's calling affects their whole life. Mine is ruled by cows, morning, noon, and night, and this shows in all my writing. Some years ago—I think it was in *Punch*—I read a verse which seems very appropriate to this late hour:

"So, when the scribbler's day of gloom comes round,
And ne'er a blessed topic can be found;
He'll write, as now I write, until I drowse,
On cows, and cows, and cows."

* * * * * *

A gentleman called to see me to-day just after lunch. He said he was on holiday in the neighbourhood, and would like to see an open-air milking outfit at work, so we walked out to mine. On our way he asked how many cows we could milk per hour. I told him about thirty, and he looked his disbelief. We found Charlie, the dairyman, just starting up. While the milking was in progress I gave my visitor some particulars as to the running of the outfit, but I expect I talked too much, I usually do, for suddenly he burst out: "I've been timing this job. There's a cow leaves the bail every 1¾ minutes. That's more than thirty per hour!" "Well," I said, "that's somewhere about what I told you." "Yes," he said, "that's the amazing part of it." "Why?" I asked. "Are we supposed to be natural liars in Wiltshire?" "No," he said, "but one expects to take off the usual trade discount for exaggeration."

It's amazing how truth flummoxes people, when they're expecting the other thing.

We watched for a bit longer, and then he said: " Your fellows aren't hurrying at all. It seems a most leisurely business, and I always thought that for a man and a lad to milk sixty cows on one of these things was sweating." Of course, he only saw the job on one pleasant afternoon. There are times in both summer and winter when the weather makes it much less of a picnic, but, on the whole, it isn't a bad job. As Charlie says: " When we'm done, we'm done. We haven't got to come back after breakfast on Sundays and clean out a cowhouse."

* * * * * *

Although you may spend your whole life in one district of our countryside, each year you will discover something new in it. The other day a neighbour introduced me to a Scotch fir tree which stands on a spur of down about a quarter of a mile south of the old road from Salisbury to Shaftesbury. This road is now a green track, but in the olden days it was the coach road to London; the old milestones can still be found by its side, and one can still trace out the ancient figures on them, giving the miles away from London. We left the car on this old track and walked across virgin downland towards a small clump of trees, two small witch elms, almost bushes, and one Scotch fir. The fir tree had a stout bough running almost at right angles to the trunk about twelve feet up, and my friend told me that it was a hanging tree, upon which our ancestors used to hang malefactors for passengers in the coaches to see. In the trunk of the tree we found the notches cut to enable the hangman to ascend the tree to fix the rope, and in the bark of the bough we could still see the marks of the rope.

And that tree is still alive, and each year it puts forth new leaves. But what tales it could tell if it could speak, and what uncomfortable moments some poor devils must have passed in that spot! Even to-day the setting of those scenes is as bleak and barren as it was two hundred years ago, and I shouldn't imagine that a dozen people visit that spot in a twelvemonth. Certainly the history of the tree was news to me, and as I looked at those rope marks while the wind blew gustily across the down, I felt cold shivers run down my back. The good old days! Maybe they were good and maybe they weren't, but somehow I prefer the days of the twentieth century with all their troubles and difficulties, and so, I expect, do most people.

There was one other feature about the setting of that tree, which was rather gruesome. The broad expanse of rolling down around it was brown and bare, but the grass underneath and immediately around that clump was bright green. Being a farmer I hunted for a reason. Why should that little circle be bright green? The reason must be a manurial one, for there was no possible chance of irrigation. Did they, horrible thought, bury the remains of the hanged underneath this natural gibbet? And, if they did, would the manurial efficacy of this persist so many years afterwards? Ugh! I hope I do not dream to-night.

* * * * * *

This is a partridge country, and to-day I had a good day's shooting through the kind offices of a friend. Birds were patchy, for the fortnight's rain in early June did a lot of damage. Occasionally we came across a strong covey of sixteen, but fours and fives and barren pairs of old birds were very frequent.

Roots were also on the scarce side, partly because of the lack of hurdled sheep and partly as a result of a dry July. But this did not matter so much as there is very little walking-up done nowadays. Which is as it should be. A walked-up partridge in September is easy game, but that same bird as he comes screwing over the down gulleys with the wind behind him takes some hitting. There was a nice breeze to-day, with the result that my own form was only moderate, but I comforted myself by remembering the way in which an old friend of my father used to judge his shooting.

He was a dear old boy, and, at the finish of a day, almost invariably ran a sweepstake on the estimate of the bag of birds, which he used to win more often than not. When asked how he reckoned the total he would reply: "There's some as shoots a deal better than me and some as shoots a damn sight worse. I keep count of my own birds. Multiply that by the number of guns, add two guns for the keeper who shoots back, and that's generally somewhere about right." And it generally was. On the same reckoning I must have been shooting up to his standard to-day. He has been dead for some years now, but how I wish that he could have been there to share the fun, and to add to it, for he was a great joker.

I can remember how annoyed my wife was when she first met him soon after we were married. He was then wearing to eighty and had a white muffler round his throat although it was a hot summer day. My wife inquired about his health, whereupon he touched the muffler and said that he had a relaxed throat which he had caught through drinking out of a damp glass. She was not used to such leg-pulling, and took this quite seriously for a moment or two until she noticed my grin and the twinkle in the old man's light-blue eyes.

Somehow I think that my generation does not get the fun out of country life and sport that our fathers did. We shoot and hunt and fish and rag our friends in much the same fashion perhaps, but modern transport has made so many more amusements available that the country ones have lost much of their importance. For instance, this evening after shooting I went to the cinema, an artificial amusement made for my pleasure by other people. My father's generation was self-sufficient. He and his shooting friends would have played penny Nap and Farmer's Glory to wind up the day. I bought my fun; they made their own; but I will admit that theirs was rather more expensive to the unlucky. Even so, they kept the money in the family, so to speak, and surely their fun had more real glory attached to it than any cinema?

* * * * * *

This notebook seems to contain very little about work this month. Harvest following immediately after haymaking robbed us of a farming breathing space in July, and so we get it in September. At least, a mainly-grass farmer such as I manages to get it, but my arable friends are as busy as ever. No sooner have they harvested one crop than they must be preparing for another. I respect their energy, but I do not envy their habit of being never done. Another thing which enables me to enjoy the countryside just now is that at long last there is a gap in my writing. I have some regular weekly stuff to do, but I have no book in hand, and can therefore take several days off in the week without giving my conscience reason to upbraid me.

This state of things is altogether delightful, for September is the month for country sport. Shooting, fishing, cub-hunting, gymkhanas, flower shows, cricket, golf, almost all the pleasures of both summer and winter are at their best. To be free at home to enjoy them to the full is, to my mind, a much better holiday than one taken away at the seaside. So, every day when I wake I say to myself, "Now what shall we do to-day?" and then proceed to do it.

Yesterday morning I rode with Pam; in the afternoon I wandered over the farm, and shot three nice young leverets and four rabbits; in the evening I went fishing; and now, after breakfast, while I am waiting for my fishing companion to arrive for a full day with the rod, seems a good chance to set down our doings on the lake last night.

There are some enormous carp in the lake, the legacy of the monks of years ago, I suppose. All the summer we had seen them splashing about like porpoises, and all the summer they had defied our efforts to catch them. I had long given them up as a bad job, but my friend is made of sterner stuff. On the way down I noticed a home-made harpoon in his car, and asked him what he proposed doing with it. " If any of those carp come sploshing up near the punt, you'll see," was his reply.

We got out on to the water about six p.m., and as this was a bit early for the evening rise we anchored in a little bay to have supper. During the meal I suddenly noticed something brown moving along the water near the shore. " Look," I whispered, pointing. " Is that an otter ? " " Golly ! " said my companion. " It's the grandfather of all the carp in the lake."

I pulled up the anchor quietly, while he got his harpoon ready. Then I paddled the punt with my hands slowly towards the fish, whilst he stood in the bows like Ajax defying the lightning, Neptune with his trident, or some mythological figure—my acquaintance with the classics is slight. Inch by inch the punt drifted towards the fish, which was rooting in the shallows for all the world like a pig. For some moments—it seemed ages—after the punt hid it from sight my companion stood poised. Then he struck, and all sorts of things happened. He had the harpoon attached to his wrist by about five yards of cord, and he seemed to be in imminent danger of following his fish into the lake.

I scrambled towards him in order to help, sending my supper and his beer into the water. " Row, you damn fool," he yelled. " Row, or we'll lose him." And lose him we did, for it takes time to get a heavy punt on the move. But he was so badly wounded that afterwards we were able to scoop him out with the net. Twenty-seven inches he measured, and fifteen pounds he weighed, but with it all he was an ugly brute. I don't suppose one ought to boast about that escapade. It probably lays us both open to prosecution, but if this takes place we can plead that it is our first offence. And I am fairly certain that it will be our last, for, having demonstrated that we can catch a carp, we shall not do any more harpooning. Such methods are not artistic enough for either of us.

Later on we caught three or four nice trout with a brown moth, and fished until long after dark, 11.30. That is the reason for this entry so soon after breakfast, for when I got home last night I was dead beat. And now, here is my harpooning friend, who is joining me for a day on the Wylye.

* * * * * *

More sport. This morning Pam and I rose long before sunrise, and long before anybody else in the house was about. She got the breakfast whilst I fed the horses, and by six o'clock we were on our way cub-hunting. As we hacked to the meet the sun peeped over the eastern ridge of down and began to disperse the mist. And from that moment the morning was pure gold.

I have long realised that I am past hunting proper, but I did not reckon that squiring a little girl during a morning's cub-hunting would be much trouble. Cub-hunting meant just hustling round and round the covers, no real riding in it—at least, this was what I told Pam.

But alas for my prophecies and my complacency! Somehow or other we worried an old fox out on to the down. Away he went; away went the hounds and the field; away, perforce, Peter took me; and away, also perforce I imagine, Toby took Pam. For several minutes I had more than I wanted in dealing

away went the hounds

with my mount, and Pam was left to take care of herself. However, when I got a chance to look round I saw Toby slithering down a grassy slope away to the left. I swung across to join him, muttering a heartfelt " Thank Heaven ! " to myself, and then we pounded on in the wake of the hunt, side by side.

We were not up at the finish, and therefore covered ourselves with no glory whatsoever, but in spite of this we had a glorious ride, and a fine sight of the pack in full cry over ten good miles of Wessex country. Then we hacked homewards, tired but happy, stopping at a pub on the way for bread and cheese and beer and lemonade. Pam may have been tired, but her appetite was in fine form.

So was her tongue. I have to be in London next week, and during my absence she wants to go cubbing with Cherub for a cavalier, all of which she explained to me at great length.

Her mother, apparently, is the stumbling-block, and she begged me to use my influence with her. I promised to do my best, and to say, which I can quite truthfully, that Cherub will be a better cavalier than I.

Then we discussed the virtues of her beloved Toby. I hinted that for hunting she required something bigger and faster in the way of mounts, but she is still faithful to her first love. The thought of selling him cannot be borne, and she is more than satisfied with the prospect of riding Toby another winter. Which is all to the good. It is better for her father's pocket and better for his mind to know that she does not want the best possible pony regardless of expense.

* * * * * *

During this month my thoughts always turn back to the harvest fields of Western Canada, especially when I hear the hum of the threshing-machine. I look at the sun-bathed stubble fields around me, and think of those seemingly endless fields of grain stooks in Manitoba, and of the men and horses there with whom I laboured twenty years ago.

Hard continuous work day after day with little or no comfort, and no amusements of any kind—by most standards such a life cannot compare with my present one. And yet, and yet, how happy I was in those days! Wherein lies the charm of that sort of life when one is young? It lies, I think, in the knowledge that one is wanted, and that one is filling a useful place in the general scheme. Hard work under those conditions is a joy. For a young man to be out of work under to-day's conditions, both here and overseas, must be horrible. To be young, and strong, and willing, and eager, and not to be allowed to run in life's race, to realise that one is not wanted—how that must hurt the soul of modern youth!

In my youth the fool, the rogue, the scallywag, or the lazy

could go abroad somewhere and find out just what they could or could not do. Now the field of adventure is woefully restricted. Other countries want no young immigrants, and our own cannot employ its young men. "Work or full maintenance" is the cry. What young man wants merely full maintenance from life? Rather he wants an opportunity to prove himself to be a man. Given that, he will be willing to take his chance about the maintenance.

In despair we listen to the planner, who is ready to plan every detail of our lives. "Full maintenance," he tells us, is easy to accomplish with proper planning, and plumes himself on his cleverness. Ye gods! Does he think men are merely pigs who want to find the trough filled three times daily? Under his system they would soon become pigs, for, to use another farming metaphor, "It takes a good horse to stand corn." Corn *ad lib.* and no work soon results in a horse that is no good to himself and a damn nuisance to everybody. If we must plan society, let us plan for a worth-while life, not just for maintenance.

And what in the dickens all that has to do with farming or Canada or September goodness knows! It just shows what happens when one lets one's pencil run away.

* * * * * *

I have been visiting an old lady who is blind, and I came away feeling both humble and grateful. Humble before such happiness in the face of calamity, and grateful to Providence that as yet I have not been similarly afflicted. She asked me how the countryside was looking, and I did my very best to try to give her a picture of it. When I mentioned the sheepfolds she said: "Ah! you can smell that. I went for a drive the other day and a whiff of it came into the car, so I got them to stop for a few moments to let me enjoy it."

Coming home I could not help thinking of this, and that blindness must be less hard to bear in the country than in the town. For in the countryside there is so much that can be " seen " with the other senses, particularly those of smelling and hearing. September is not so fragrant as June, but it grants a few scents and many sounds of its own as one walks abroad. The rasp of the plough as it grates along the furrow, the jingle of the traces, the scent of the newly-turned earth, the sound of the huntsman's horn, the popping of the shot-guns, the whirr of the driven partridge, the wet flop against one's gaiters as one walks through a root field, the flip, flip, of the stubble against one's boots, the scent of sheepfolds, of late hay, and of the dust around the threshing-machine or in the barn when barley is being winnowed.

God forbid that I should ever lose the precious gift of sight while I live ; but, should such a calamity befall me, I shall pray that I may continue to live in the country. For there my nose and ears will enable me still to enjoy the pageant of England's countryside during its stately passage from one year's end to another.

* * * * * *

There seems to be no end to the joys of this September. To-day I accepted an invitation from my very good friends, the water-keepers, to help them drag the river for coarse fish, and great fun it was. Pam, to her great sorrow, was booked to spend the day elsewhere, so my wife and I, or rather the old people, set off to try to recapture one of the thrills of years ago. Old clothes, the most charming of hosts, and a golden September day in the meadows, what more could one desire ?

We helped to pull the nets, we sploshed in the mud, we got our feet and most of our legs thoroughly wet, we mourned when a large pike escaped the net, and exulted when such a fish was captured. We shared the keepers' lunch, so shyly and so courteously offered; we talked with them; we listened to their talk—valuable stuff, for this type of countryman is sparing with words; and we admired and appreciated their efficiency. Never did they hurry, but always they did the right thing just at the right time.

It is difficult to square the argument that blood sports have a brutalising influence on those who engage in them with the character and behaviour of the average keeper, either of land or water. Always I have found them to be exceptionally gentle and courteous, and for their help in my rural education I shall be ever grateful. They, more than anybody, taught me the value of patience, of perseverance, and of good manners. I always feel proud when they invite me to their September revel of dragging the river, for this is something which cannot be purchased with money. If you don't fit into the rural jigsaw it does not come your way.

My wife—she is a miller's daughter—thoroughly enjoyed herself to-day. The meadows and the river and the mud and the genial company and the sunshine went to her head like fine champagne, and so excited was she that I was moved to suggest that before long she would be in the river, head and ears. Whereupon she deserted me for a stalwart young keeper of her acquaintance, and proceeded to enjoy herself thoroughly; leaving me, a less adventurous spirit, to chat with the head keeper.

"We'd be badly off wi'out Mrs. Street," this worthy remarked, as he watched her hauling on a rope like an able seaman. "An' ain't she 'appy? Don't look much mor'n zixteen." A pretty compliment indeed, for her flushed cheeks were daubed with mud, and her skirt, although a short one, was an undeniable Dorothy Draggle-tail.

But by the finish, three p.m., both of us realised two things. Firstly, that we were three good miles from home; and secondly,

A farm Sale

that we were dog-tired, and considerably older than sixteen. Still, if you know your way about, there is always a *modus vivendi* in the countryside. The keepers had presented us with two huge pike, and we used one of these as currency with which to purchase transport. We called on some friends and presented them with one of the fish; whereupon they gave us tea and afterwards drove us home.

* * * * * *

How the time slips by! Already the local papers are filled with advertisements of farm sales, and to-day I attended one, where I bought ten in-calf heifers and a thatching ladder. It occurs to me that there are few farms in this district which I have not visited to attend a dispersal sale. And I am only forty-three! It just shows that even in the countryside few men stay put for many years.

But the land remains. That thought came to me once again as I topped a ridge of down on my way home and saw the Wylye valley spread out before me in all its quiet beauty. And then I thought that " remains " was the wrong word, in that it draws a picture of death. The land never dies. It lives on while generations of men are born and die and sink into oblivion. "Persists" is the word—the land "persists," no matter what men may do.

Attending that farm sale has made me realise that I have persisted with this notebook for a full farming year; and yet it seems but a few weeks ago that I resolved to begin this wayward scribbling. It cannot be called a diary; it has no settled purpose behind it, and it obeys no formula save my own mood at the time; but on glancing through it I seem to find a little of the real flavour of this part of Wilts. Surely that should tell me that it was worth the trouble? Shall I continue with it to-morrow, which is October once more, and the beginning of yet another farming year? Somehow I think I will do so, for it does not take much time, and during these twelve short months it has become a habit, whether good or bad is not for me to say.

But whether I do so or not is immaterial. Farming goes on. Other men have written diaries. Some of these have lived after them and some have not. Some men have farmed well; others have farmed badly. Statesmen have made speeches; clever planners have evolved wonderful plans. Inventors invent, towns are built, and mankind does all sorts of wonderful things. But farming goes on amidst it all. It is the one stable industry. The land persists. Townsmen, put that in your pipes and smoke it if you can.

To-morrow English farming begins yet another year. A very small cog in its complicated mechanism here wishes it God-speed.